More Acclaim for Conquering Deception...

"A mountain of information about human behavior. You'll learn when you might be being deceived—and, better yet, you'll learn how to control the situation when you aren't ready to be totally forthcoming. An indispensable book for doing business in the zeroes."

—Christopher Null, **SMART BUSINESS MAGAZINE**

"*Conquering Deception* is a powerful translation of the best police interview techniques, ready to lend the inside track in every business, social, or personal conversation—this is the definitive handbook for savvy communication."

—Detective John J. Clark, **NYPD** (Ret.)

"While there are many books on lying, this one is unique. Not only does Mr. Nance's considerable experience jump out of every page, it is written in a style bound to capture the reader."

—Joseph T. Wells, CFE, CPA, **THE WHITE PAPER**

"Whether hillbilly or millionaire, each of us is impacted by our conversations with others. Think you're hearing everything that's being said? Read *Conquering Deception* and hear what you've been missing."

—Max Baer, Jr., **ACTOR/PRODUCER/DIRECTOR**
(*"Jethro Bodine"* - The Beverly Hillbillies)

"Fascinating. Jef Nance translates his years of law enforcement experience into common sense advice that can help everyone become a better judge of character and a better communicator."

—J. Peder Zane, **THE NEWS AND OBSERVER**,
Raleigh, North Carolina

"Persistence is more powerful than talent."

—*Calvin L. Hutton*

Conquering Deception

SECOND EDITION
Edited by Frank Barton Hill

Jef Nance, CFE

I·B

IRVIN-BENHAM • KANSAS CITY

Published in the Unites States of America by Irvin-Benham, LLC,
P. O. Box 11806, Kansas City, Missouri 64138.
e/mail: ibgroup@kcnet.com

author e/mail: cdauthor@hotmail.com

Library of Congress Control Number: 00-132447
ISBN 0-9672862-4-7

SECOND EDITION
Printed in the Unites States of America

To Missy...
long lost, found at last.

Acknowledgments

Because nothing much gets done without the help of others, I wish to extend my deepest thanks to the following people, and in no particular order: Alan W. Foust, Walt Waggoner, Bonnie J. Freeland, Cal Fussman (Contributing Editor, *Esquire Magazine*), Christopher Null (Executive Editor, *Smart Business Magazine*), Rieva Lesonsky (Editorial Director, *Entrepreneur Magazine*), Mary Shtohryn, Steve "The Torpedo" Santoli, Bryan Crites, Paul Maccabee, Berta Nance, K. J. Hunter, Frank Barton Hill, Trevor A. Noisworthy, J. Peder Zane (Book Review Editor, *The News and Observer*-Raleigh, North Carolina), Marla Markman (Managing Editor, *Entrepreneur Magazine*), Joseph T. Wells, CFE, CPA (Chairman, Association of Certified Fraud Examiners), Terry Behrens, Max Baer, Jr., and John J. Clark—to my father, Loel F. Nance, for his authentic storytelling, and to my mother, Mary Ann Nance.

And to God, from whom it all originates.

Contents

Introduction

Part I
Calibration

Part II
Verbal Voodoo

Part III
Tone, Taste, Tenacity

Introduction

Have you ever listened to a person and suspected they were lying? When that happened, did you realize what made you question their honesty? Did you have a reliable method for judging truthfulness in conversation, or was it merely gut instinct that tapped you on the shoulder and caused you to wonder about that person's veracity?

To varying degrees, most people can sense deception. Some are better at it than others. But even those who have the knack for detecting deceit may still dismiss their conclusions because they realize they have no real method for reaching them. Suspicion is a first step, not an answer. If gut instinct is all one has to rely on, suspicion can quickly turn to aggravation and then to self-doubt—*was he really lying...or wasn't he?*

Our teachers covered reading, writing, and arithmetic until we were dizzy—but they never taught us how to navigate with proficiency in conversation. Knowing how to diagram a sentence doesn't serve us too well when we're buying a used car, speaking with a boss or subordinate, or trying to communicate with our spouse. It is ironic, even sad, that we put such great effort into educating ourselves to do so many things, but put absolutely no effort into learning how to decipher what others have said, and how to speak so that our ideas and beliefs are accepted by them. When we venture out into the world we find that we can put none of our formal education into action without conversing with another person. Everything we do relies upon the spoken word. And in the real world, the person who is the most insightful and savvy will have the upper hand in *any* conversation.

As an interrogator, I used the principles in this book to get confessions from criminal suspects. When I moved into undercover work, I took them with me and used them to manage informants and gain the trust of drug dealers. As a trooper, I used them during traffic stops where they enabled me to interdict hundreds of pounds of marijuana and cocaine on the highways. I was fortunate to learn these techniques early on in my career, and I brought them with me and adapted them as I moved into new arenas. In every situation, my position of authority took a backseat to something far more powerful: the words that I listened to, and the words that I spoke.

My goal here, through the powerful but little known principles of the police interrogation room, is to bring some science to your gut instinct. Instead of simply having that old "feeling" that you're missing the real story in a conversation, I want you to be able to judge the veracity of others and know how you did it—and have confidence that you are right in your judgment.

From losing weight to getting rich, recipes for quick solutions abound. Though we spend our lives chasing them, the truth is that in nearly every instance, shortcuts are an illusion. Ultimately, we must admit to ourselves that proficiency or success in any endeavor is directly proportionate to effort. That's certainly true with becoming adept in the art of recognizing deception. Learn all you can from credible sources and then test that knowledge in some fashion every day. Without your continuing analysis of people, the valuable information presented in the following pages is certain to erode away.

Have you ever watched a movie a second time and noticed something you missed in the first viewing? If you'll take my advice, you may have a similar experience when you read this book. Studying how to do something can be far different from actually doing it. How many of us could rebuild the motor of a 1948 Harley Davidson after reading the service manual one time? People are not machines, but they can be just as complex—and even less predictable. I recommend that you read this book, then watch and listen to people for a month. Then come back and read it again. Like a great movie, I'm confident it will have even more meaning and clarity the second time around.

Part I

Calibration

Realizing There's More

On December 18, 1922, Oklahoma bank robber Harvey Bailey led a daring daylight robbery of the Denver Mint that netted him and his band of outlaws more than $200,000. Though the feat seems un-believable today, the Denver robbery was sandwiched into a long line of successful and lucrative bank jobs pulled by the Bailey Gang in the Midwest throughout the 1920's. Considered the dean of American bank robbers by crime historians, Bailey had a reputation for metic-ulously planning the jobs his group undertook. In selecting his prospective targets, he would assess the financial worth of a town, determine the locations of traffic policemen, calculate the precise time allowable inside the bank, and make certain to strike when the stores of money were at their maximum. In his book *John Dillinger Slept Here*, crime historian Paul Maccabee writes, "Who else but Harvey Bailey would think to obtain road maps from the county surveyor's office to ensure that the roads were adequate for a perfect getaway?" Harvey Bailey, in short, was big on strategy.

Harvey Bailey's approach to crime sharply contrasts to that of the typical criminal, then and today. Over the course of a dozen years in law enforcement, I found that the overwhelming majority of the people committing crimes today are not calculating criminal masterminds, but short-sighted opportunists guided more by impulse than logic. The lure of immediate (and often meager) gains overshadows every other consideration, and in their haste, they fail to adequately plan ahead. There may be no greater example of this than a case I worked in which a man burgled his neighbor's house and then tracked through six inches of fresh snow with his take, right up to his own back doorstep. How would you rate this man's escape preparations against those of Harvey Bailey?

Because they lack strategy and forethought, many repeat offenders end up going to prison and doing what we used to call "life on the installment plan": three years here, five there, and so on, always for crimes that produced no lasting fruit. In the end, most have nothing but bad tattoos and memories of penitentiary life to show for it all.

If you think education is expensive, try ignorance.
—Derek Bok

Just as criminals succeed or fail in direct proportion to the amount of strategy they use, so do the rest of us. The average citizen who ignores strategy may not go to prison in the strict sense of the word, but he may doom himself to something much akin to it—a life of mediocrity, of just paying the bills, of being merely average. Like the criminal who bumbles along reacting to what comes his way without regard to the long term, most people amble through life without any real plan, simply accepting what comes along and adapting in small ways to only stay afloat.

Thinking is the hardest work there is, which is probably the reason so few engage in it.

—Henry Ford

Great accomplishments don't just happen. We know the names of Orville and Wilbur Wright, Henry Ford, and Bill Gates, because these were people who broke from conventional wisdom to turn their ideas into realities. They didn't plod along aimlessly. They envisioned the outcomes they wanted and they used planning to achieve them. Whether we want to climb Mount Everest, create the next Microsoft, or communicate with a commanding edge, we'll have to do it with strategy.

Strategic Conversation

The mention of strategy and conversation in the same sentence should seem about as logical as using a term like "hectic relaxation." With strategy comes planning, organization, and discipline. Conversation, we've all come to believe, has none of that. Dictionaries, in fact, use words like "informal" in defining it. Conversations can ramble and meander, taking us in unpredictable directions. The greatest part about them may be that while the rest of our lives seem to be encumbered by structure and limitations, conversation generally comes with neither. Strategy and conversation, it would seem, should have little in common.

Why, then, have the two been brought together here? To

answer that, we first need to establish what the term conversation really includes. Take a look at the following choices and note the one(s) that you would consider to fall under the umbrella of conversation:

1) job interview
2) counseling session with your subordinate/boss
3) telling your neighbor to keep his dog off your yard
4) speaking with a police officer as he writes you a ticket
5) visiting with Uncle John on Thanksgiving Day

Most everyone would readily agree that #5 should be considered conversation, but what about the other four? Does a situation necessarily have to be comfortable or friendly in order to be considered conversation? Is true conversation only made of lemonade, front porches, and good friends? Not necessarily.

Though the first four situations may be unpleasant ones, they involve at least two people who are exchanging thoughts, directions, questions, or ideas, and because of this, they all can be considered conversation. Explained this way, it's evident that virtually every verbal encounter we have with another person is a conversation—whether we're buying a hamburger or a new car, trying for a new job, expressing our dissatisfaction to a salesclerk, or giving courtroom testimony, we are *conversing*.

The next consideration is, "How do we approach conversation if we're serious about understanding what is *truly* being said to us, and serious about getting greater acceptance from others of what we have to say?" If conversation encompasses every facet of our lives, wouldn't a thinking person want to be good at it? Sadly, the average person stumbles through life relying on his gut feeling to determine whether people are being genuine with him and allowing his emotions to dictate how he will relate his thoughts to others.

At work or home, conversation impacts our successes and our failures. It encompasses absolutely every part of our lives, and no one is exempt. With regard to dealing with fellow gangsters, Harvey Bailey once said, "It's all done by word of mouth. Writing is out—o-u-t." Even legendary bank robbers depended on conversation.

Revelations

Until recent years, the idea of teaching front line, uniformed cops how to talk to people never surfaced. Of everything that a cop does on a day-to-day basis, talking to people is the common thread that runs through all of it. How to talk to people, and just as importantly, how to watch, listen to, and evaluate them, remains one of the most overlooked pieces of study in law enforcement academies throughout the United States.

Over the years I came to realize this very obvious fact—law enforcement is a "people business." Traffic accidents. Domestic disputes. Taking information for incident reports. Giving directions. Regardless of the situation, efficient communication (in both directions) comes into play. Ironically, I never saw it addressed in training. The traditional attitude has been that cops need to know the laws, how to handle themselves in a tussle, and how to shoot. There's the paperwork, too, which will be learned on the job. But how to talk? The Old School cops would have laughed that off: "This is how you talk—you tell him how it's gonna be. If he gives you any static, you give him a mouth fulla dirt."

But when I think back to the fights we got into during police calls, I realize that most of them were preceded by conversation, albeit sometimes brief. What would happen was invariably affected by what we, the officers, said. Our demeanor, the tone with which we delivered our directions, even the people we issued them in front of, influenced outcomes of situations. Tell a guy in front of half a dozen of his buddies that he's going to do "X" or else and see what happens. You've put his pride on the line. Some of the officers I worked with, some good friends of mine, just had a natural way of upping the ante. We all knew who could escalate things into a fight on a disturbance call—they seldom let us down.

As the years passed, my approach changed. I talked more. I listened more. If I went on a call where someone's brother-in-law was refusing to leave, I'd rely more on conversation to accomplish the mission than I might have previously. I found this new way to be even more entertaining than the old one. I suppose it was a kind of wit-matching with these people, which became more interesting (and less tiring) to me than, for instance, saying, "Leave right now. Did you say no?" *Whack, umph, cuff.*

Of course, we have to be realistic. Being diplomatic won't always work. There are a certain number of people out there who, in certain situations, just can't be reasoned with. For them the outcome would be the same regardless of how we conversed; they weren't going to be happy unless they made a scene and went to jail.

My fellow officers and I were dealing with eccentric, if not difficult, people on a regular basis. Given a little room, many of them could be quite entertaining. When I get together now with old friends from those days I realize the stories we share came from the people on the street, characters beyond the imagination of the best fiction writers. There was Tin Can Gene, Turnaround (AKA "Eat 'em up"), The Widder George, The King Black Joker, "Melon" Williams, Merlin the Magician...the cast was a big one. It was what these people said, how they looked, their mannerisms—all their eccentricities—that made them so memorable. The extreme and raw variety of people one encounters on the job is a big part of what makes police work so fascinating.

APPROACH AND DELIVERY

A few months after my twenty-second birthday, I hit the streets with a gun on my hip. Suddenly I was everybody's daddy. I'm telling people my parents' age what to do now. And they're going to do just what I say because I'm The Law. Sure. I never really expected that, and after being on the job a while I knew why. I came to understand that what I said, and more importantly, how I said it, was vital to getting the outcomes I wanted. That was the power. I knew there was a way. I began to use strategy.

They say you learn by doing, but I believe that you can sometimes learn even more by watching others. It's hard to be a player and a judge at the same time. Mistakes and successes can be much easier to evaluate when you're sitting on the sidelines.

Occasionally, a day shift lieutenant would get a light bulb over his head and send us out to clean up the streets. We would be handed pages of names, people wanted because they had failed to show up for a dinner date with the city judge. This was considered a grunt detail and the efforts usually met with little success. These people move frequently, sleep late, and in rare instances, work during the daytime.

On one of these outings, I happened to be paired with another officer who was known as being strictly by the book. By that I only mean that he lacked creativity, which is a necessity for a street officer. Within the bounds of the law, exceptionally great cops use some ingenuity from time to time. We went to several houses and each time he would start off with something like this: "Good morning, we've got a warrant for Jerome's arrest. Is he here?"

I want to point out now that you'll likely find things in this book that you already know. Even so, you may find that you never *realized* that you knew them. That was the case with me as I watched this officer. When I heard him using this approach, I knew instantly what was wrong with it, and I benefitted from seeing him do it. It caused me to acknowledge something I had always known but had failed to really capitalize upon. My words were powerful; how I chose them and how I transmitted them would bring me success or failure.

We had been to a dozen houses without a single arrest. In fairness to this officer, I have to mention that it can be hard to get a wanted man to come to the door when two cops are standing on the porch. But people don't always make good decisions under pressure. We had the element of surprise on our side, and the uniforms are certainly unnerving to some people—particularly the ones who have a wanted man lurking in a room behind them. Fortunately for us, it was oftentimes the girlfriend, wife, or mother of a suspect that answered our knock. She had to make fast decisions. She had to look believable. She was never trained to do either. Her weakness was our opportunity, but opportunity, of course, has to be seized or it slips away.

As we walked up to the next house, I happened to be ahead of him, and this time I was first to the door. I knocked and a ratty-haired woman of about forty answered. In a confident manner I said, "Good morning, we need to see Alvin." There was silence. She waited for me to speak again (probably because she didn't know what to say), and I stared at her as if I knew he was inside.

The woman had a dilemma. It hinged on her impression that I knew Alvin was in the house. By phrasing the statement this way, I had skipped right over the question of *whether* he was in the house. My words assumed his presence. The majority of people I confronted with this approach said, "Just a minute," and then took us to "Alvin." That's just what this woman did.

A few months later I was paired with the same officer for the warrant detail. We had never discussed the difference in our approaches, so I had no feel for whether he had picked up on it. There had been many things—good and bad—that I had learned from the officers around me, and I was interested to see whether he was still introducing himself the way he always had. We pulled up to the curb in front of the first address on the list and I let him take the lead: "Hi, we've got an arrest warrant for Randy. Is he here?" At least you could count on this man for consistency.

We must constantly be observant of the failures and successes in conversation around us and adjust our strategies accordingly. Our own failures are often costly and our own successes take time to accumulate. The most expedient way to learn what works and what doesn't is through observing our fellow man. We can learn from his mistakes without paying the price for failure ourselves, and reap the lessons of his successes without the time consuming trial and error he went through.

Learn from the mistakes of others. You can't live long enough to make them all yourself.

—Eleanor Roosevelt

Whatever our station in life, there are examples of failure and success, both large and small, occurring around us continually. They should be treated as a resource. We should recognize them, evaluate them, pluck what's valuable from them, and put what we learn to work.

Realization and evaluation are at the root of every piece of knowledge that we have today. We realize something in nature and we evaluate how it lives. We realize a problem and we evaluate a solution. We realize a necessity, and we evaluate a way to fill it with invention.

Getting really good at conversation is no different. Most people listen and speak instinctively—or worse yet, emotionally—rather than logically. Impulse guides them, not intellect, and their frustrations and failures are endless because of this. Few ever figure out what was the cause or what could have been the solution of their shortcomings. They never realize that it's possible to get so much more meaning from what others say, and so much more effect out of what we say ourselves. Having that simple realization is half the battle in becoming a shrewd conversationalist.

Lying vs. Deception…Is There A Difference?

From an early age we've all known what it is to lie. Never to do it is undoubtedly one of the first lessons that any good parent tries to bestow upon their child. We want our children to be trustworthy, honest and respectable, and just as importantly, we want others to perceive them as being trustworthy, honest and respectable. We understand that how we are perceived by those around us is based upon what we say and do, and that being perceived as a liar strips us of credibility. A person without credibility will have a hard time building relationships or a progressive path to success. To a large extent, our credibility is built upon our believability—lying undermines both.

It's a cruel paradox, then, that for as long as we've been told not to lie, we've come into one situation after another in which a lie seems to be an attractive remedy. The truth can be ugly, embarrassing, or incriminating, and a lie can be anything we want it to be. The little devil on our shoulder is constantly scanning for the easiest route, but not necessarily the most ethical or prudent one. The search for a solution may end with deciding to lie.

A lie can come in a multitude of shapes and sizes, with just as many underlying motivations. Though the term has a negative connotation, a lie may not necessarily be destructive or insidious. Situations can arise wherein lying may be the "right" thing to do. If a friend proudly waltzed into the room wearing a gaudy pink and blue gown and too much rouge, what would you say if she asked your opinion of her appearance? The truth? That she looked awful? No, you would tell a lie, arguably a more decent thing to do in such a case than telling the truth. Of course you would want to spare her feelings, but wouldn't you be partly motivated to lie in this instance because telling the truth would be more difficult and uncomfortable for you? You would be taking the easiest route for both of you.

In most cases, however, lies are told for less noble reasons. We lie about money to make ourselves look more successful, or about running into a traffic jam so that we don't have to admit oversleeping, or about being at Ronnie's house when the shooting went down at Danny's house. We want to look good in the eyes of others. We want to dodge blame. We want to avoid admitting our bad deeds. Lies are a tempting option, ready in a moments notice to cover for us.

So whether one lies to avoid rubbing another person the wrong way, or about where they went last night, all lies share this commonality: they are overt untrue statements. They require action. In order to lie, one must actually generate a falsehood and then put it out for consumption.

Deception, on the other hand, can occur with much less effort. While a lie demands that an untrue statement be made, deception requires only that one mislead, which is a much broader proposition that, upon examination, we'll find actually wields a lot more power. Depending upon the situation, a person can mislead by:

- avoiding the issue
- omitting the truth from what he says
- letting an untrue statement of another person go uncorrected, or
- use of the most aggressive form of deception, lying

That's right, lying is merely a type of deception. If deception were the whole kingdom of trees with all species within it, then lying would be just one kind of tree—the Giant Redwood, probably.

Circumstance, personality, and combinations of both determine whether a person will be deceptive, lie, or do neither. Some folks are intrinsically honest, regardless of situational demands. There are "latent liars," people who normally avoid being deceptive, but will be in the right situation. Then there are the intrinsically dishonest. One person might say to a clerk who had returned too much change, "You gave me an extra twenty," and hand it back. Another might say nothing if the clerk failed to catch it, and yet another might deny receiving the money even if the clerk suspicioned it and quizzed him.

Though our folks talked about the misfortunes of lying, they probably didn't say much about deception, which is more powerful and more prevalent. It's both of these because there are many who don't have the nerve to look someone in the eye and tell an outright lie but feel quite comfortable merely misleading them.

Imagine that Burton leaves work one day and on the way home swings by the Red Baron for a quick beer. When he gets to the house late, his wife Ruby asks, "Did you go by the bar again on the way home?" "Honey," he says, "there was the longest line at the post office, and I thought I'd never get out of there. Here are the stamps you wanted." Did he lie? No. There really was a line at the post office—when he went there during his lunch hour. Was he deceptive? Certainly. He led his wife to believe that he hadn't gone to the bar. He misled her by pointing to an irrelevant truth and omitting the pertinent one.

Most people have a natural aversion to lying, and the reasons for this have to do less with conscience than with self-preservation. Though a lie can be an immediate fix, the fear of being caught can dissuade a person from issuing one. Too, even when there is no foreseeable threat of being caught, there's something frightening about confining oneself to a specific story.

A person who lies commits himself to an assertion that can be examined, compared against, and attacked. That's why even a seasoned liar will try some milder form of deception initially. He wades in gradually, only going deeper if he has to. Typically, there comes a point when a deceptive person in a protracted act of deceit finds himself at a crossroads. The risk is increasing and a decision must be made. He can retreat and distance himself from his previous assertions if things have gotten too messy for his tastes, or he can plunge full ahead until he finds himself telling a lie.

Part of what makes deception so popular over outright lying is its versatility. With deception, there's some ambiguity left in what is said. The speaker doesn't have to pin himself down irrevocably. Deception is tight enough to satisfy, but loose enough that one may still salvage himself if the situation unravels.

What if the next day Ruby runs into Midge, who reports that she saw Burton coming out of the Red Baron last evening?

Depending upon how much stomach he's got for this kind of sport (or how big Ruby's rolling pin is), Burton will have several options when she confronts him:

1) truthful: "Okay, honey, I stopped by the bar for a few minutes. I'm sorry."
2) bargaining: "She might have seen me drive past the bar."
3) referencing: "I told you where I went."
4) attacking: "Midge is nuts. She's trying to cause problems for us."
5) lying: "I came straight home, honey."

When it comes to high places, it's not the fall that hurts, it's the landing. The same can be said for lying; it's only dangerous when you get caught. If Burton uses line #1, we can assume that his fear of being caught outweighs his desire to get away with this stunt, so he abandons the deception process immediately.

Notice also that even as Burton does the uncommon thing of owning up, he still couches it with "for a few minutes," an addendum that's meant to minimize his conduct.

When Burton uses line #2, he's continuing the deception, but feeling things out. He's not sure how solid the evidence is. He's bargaining, throwing out a small concession that might explain away what Midge saw. He hopes that this will pacify Ruby and relieve him from having to proceed toward an outright lie.

If Burton uses line #3, he'll be in good company. Everyone from political figures to criminal suspects can be heard making remarks like, "I've told you before," "I think you know my position on that," "I've answered that question fully and honestly," or "I'm not going to go through it again." Our natural reluctance to lie is so strong that rather than repeat a deceptive statement, a person will often just point back to one.

With line #4, Burton would be stepping the game up a notch. Without addressing any part of the actual issue, he deflects the accusation by attacking the accuser, a common defensive move of the guilty.

If Burton opts for line #5, he's committed himself to a lie, and if proven wrong, will sustain maximum damage to his credibility. Again, the best part of deception is the wiggle-room that it allows, and with this outright lie Burton will leave himself absolutely none.

The deception of Burton's possible responses generally increases from #2 to #5. When confronted with the news of Midge's sighting, Burton could go with any one of these, or start anywhere on the scale and up the ante as he's pressed. Again, if he's like most people, he'll use the least deception necessary to get the job done. Through #4, if found out, he might still manage to somehow save face. But by the time he gets to #5, he's locked himself in, and he'll be cast a liar when Ruby finds the dated lottery ticket from the Red Baron in his pants pocket.

For those who choose deception, we must consider a second factor—how far will he go to support or defend his misrepresentation? Just as people have a threshold at which they will become deceptive, most then have another threshold at which they will rescind or abandon the deception.

For some that threshold is low. Such was the case with a young man I met at the scene of a burglary one morning. He greeted me as I got out of my patrol car. He walked alongside me up the driveway and gave me an overview of the burglary scene and what had been taken. A next door neighbor to the victim, he said he had been gone the previous night. He added that his wife had reported that the dogs didn't bark and she had heard no noises. He would have gone into the house with me when the elderly victim opened the door, but I asked him to wait outside.

As I walked through the house, I noticed something unusual on the carpet. I knelt down for a closer look: *wax*. Suddenly I saw them everywhere—little dots of red wax dripped from a candle as the burglar made his rounds though a dark house.

Back outside, the neighbor shadowed me again as I walked around the exterior of the house. He talked continually. *He was too helpful.* I have joked on occasion that people who are overly friendly make me uncomfortable—situations like this one are what have given me that predisposition. I looked up from my clipboard and stared at his face: he lives next door...he made a point of telling me he had been away the evening of the burglary...*his eyebrows are singed*!

Suddenly I felt like listening to this guy. After a few minutes of conversation I asked with a slight show of concern, "What happened to your eyebrows?" He rubbed them, but didn't speak immediately. "Oh, I was lighting a cigarette on the stove," he offered after a moment. He was obviously a little off-balance, so I followed up with a left cross: "If someone told me they saw you outside your house last night, what would you say to that?" He turned ashen. "Why, did somebody say that?" he asked. Minutes later, right there in the victim's yard, he confessed to the crime.

This fellow was not a career criminal, he was an opportunist with poor judgment. When his story was questioned, he backed away from it quickly. Ironically, it was less stressful for him to come clean than to go forward down the path of deception. Others, though, won't be so timid.

On another occasion, I worked a case in which a forged check had been cashed at a supermarket. An automated camera at the counter had snapped a clear black and white photo of the suspect as he slid the check to the cashier. During the interrogation of the suspect, I presented the picture. He studied it. He looked at the back, then flipped to the front again. I was ready for the confession that was sure to come next when suddenly he said, "That's not me." With his forefinger pressed to the photograph, he said confidently, "I don't own a shirt like that."

Did this man have an aversion to taking responsibility for his actions? Absolutely, such that it allowed him to lie even when confronted with evidence that no reasonable person would try to explain away. Most suspects at that point would have acknowledged defeat, said nothing, or simply asked for an attorney. But his way out was to deny owning a shirt like the one in the picture, despite the clear shot of his face. A small percentage of people will cling to their lies even in the face of ironclad contradictory evidence. They consider "the necessity of deception" to be so great that they aren't bothered by the absurdity of their denials.

Deception poses a greater threat to us because it's much easier to do than lying, and because more people find themselves able to do it. Since many instances permit deception with such little effort—sometimes by doing absolutely nothing—it's an easier thing to perpetrate both in practice and in conscience. Fans of *The Andy Griffith Show* will remember the episode in which Andy and Barney were trying to gain membership into the very elite Esquire Club at Mount Pilot. So that they might appear more worldly, Barney suggested to Andy that they mention the stock market. "We don't own any stocks," Andy said. Barney shook his head. "All you have to do is say, 'I noticed U.S. Steel went up three points today,' and look happy about it," he explained. "That ain't lyin'." Barney was right; it was deception.

So when our parents told us not to lie, they really didn't cover the subject adequately. And while many profess to teach methods for ferreting out the liars, I submit that those efforts aren't adequate, either, since the liars among us are vastly outnumbered by the deceivers. Learn to detect deception and spotting the liars will become a natural and effortless by-product of your talent.

Part II

verbal voodoo

The Foundations Of Influence

The recipes for success are many and varied, but the best ones share a simple idea: command of the spoken word and the ability to influence other people are key in getting ahead. What could make more sense? Those who can communicate well not only have the power to relate their ideas understandably, but to charge others with the enthusiasm it takes to turn them into reality. We can't achieve much standing alone. Whether they've recognized it this plainly or not, successful people in every kind of endeavor have been forced to deal with an unavoidable truth, that to achieve what we want, we will need the assistance of other people.

The subjects of human relations, reading body language, and even detecting deception are typically lumped into the category of communication. To be specific, though, what we're really talking about is conversation. While they all may be *forms* of communication, it's in the context of conversation that they occur. Everything we involve ourselves in, from marriages to corporate mergers, is furthered or failed through conversation. It's the medium through which deception is carried out and also the one where we can most effectively influence the behavior, decisions, or beliefs of others.

This chapter and the next will address influence, because many of the techniques that enable us to influence others also put us in position to detect deception. Though seldom discussed together, influence and detecting deception are intrinsically connected and well worth studying in tandem.

Before getting into the subject of influence, it should be explained just what that term does and doesn't mean in this context. While putting a revolver to the head of another person might result in him doing what you want, it won't likely bring him to *believe* in what he's doing. He will not have been influenced, he will have been coerced. As soon as the threat is gone, so will be his cooperation. Our aim isn't merely to get people to do or think something because we believe in it, but to get them to do or think it because they believe in it themselves. Since we all tend to put our own interests above those of others, isn't it quite obvious that we'll get more cooperation, motivation, or production from another person when he believes in the mission at hand? Won't he work harder for a cause he believes in, than one he's commanded to take on? Our ability to get others to see something our way by allowing them to see it themselves has tremendous power and potential.

Leadership is the art of getting someone else to do something you want done because he wants to do it.

—President Dwight D. Eisenhower

Just as influence should not come through force, neither should it come through trickery, which is itself on an equal moral plane with deception. It's not necessary to be shifty or underhanded in order to bring people to agreement with us, it's only necessary that we take care in choosing our words and how we say them. Though it may be a very effective means of influence—and a popular one as well—the art of trickery and manipulation is one that's short lived. When a person is found to be manipulative (or worse, becomes known for it), his credibility will suffer or die altogether.

When confronted with someone who opposes our point of view, each of us reacts in our own way. Many variables will impact how we handle such situations, including our individual personality, knowledge of the subject, relationship to the opponent, and who else is present listening and watching. The instinctive thing to do is resort to argument and the easiest thing to do is walk away (literally or figuratively) from these challenges. But as we'll see, neither argument nor retreat stand much chance of getting our message accepted.

The real art of influence has two facets: 1) bringing another person to our way of thinking, and 2) doing it so that our efforts are not readily apparent. No one should realistically expect to fix a car engine by beating it with a hammer, but people commonly deal with opposing opinions in a way that's strikingly similar. We tend to want to verbally beat our message into the opposing person until they see things our way. This is an ineffective way to affect influence, largely because it arouses the ego of the other person, and it makes apparent that we are trying to change their point of view.

Anyone who has been in the "real world" already knows that in many ways it really is "every man for himself." Does that present an obstacle to dealing with others? That depends upon whether this fact is considered or ignored. The key to getting what we want from others is in the way we package and present our ideas. Too often we're focused solely on our own objectives, with disregard for the interests of the people we want to influence.

A good salesman knows that he can't expect to make a sale based upon what he wants. The potential customer won't be influenced to buy because the salesman announces he's falling behind in his numbers for the month, that he's saving to buy a new fishing boat, or even that he has a baby to feed. If these are the reasons he gives as to why someone should buy his vacuum cleaner, how many do you think he'll sell? What if, on the other hand, he explains the exemplary features of the Cleveland Vacuum, its lifetime guarantee, its storable size, its economical price tag, and how its ease of operation will make life simpler for the prospective customer? Doesn't it seem logical that a prospect will be more likely to buy a Cleveland when he realizes the many ways this machine will benefit him?

Incorporating this line of thinking into our everyday lives can bring about astounding results. In the process of helping others gain what they want, oftentimes our own objectives are fulfilled as well.

The Three Cornerstones Of Influence

Unlike the surly television detectives, I've found that it's much easier to ferret out the truth through cooperation than confrontation. When people are comfortable, they talk more. They open up. They drop their guard. The symptoms of deception then become more abundant and easier to read.

In many situations, our ability to recognize another person's deception will be dependent on our ability to make them comfortable with us and confident in us. To that end, there are three basic and powerful attributes that I've found to be indispensable in accomplishing both: credibility, rapport, and respect.

CREDIBILITY

One of the greatest assets any of us can hope to possess is credibility. It's our key to the world. It can bring prestige, money, friendship, respect, and a long list of other benefits to the holder. Credibility inspires the trust of those around you; its value cannot be overstated.

The Credibility Continuum. We're all blessed with "presumed credibility." Despite the skeptical or even cynical predisposition that some of us might have, we still presume that our fellow man is truthful, and therefore credible, and our fellow man presumes that we are, too. This general presumption is perfectly intact until we see a person, hear him speak, or watch his behavior. If he falters in the process of doing any one of these, that presumed credibility is diminished or destroyed.

Physical appearance has tremendous impact on credibility. When it comes to first impressions, the way a person looks is the real one. We're generally viewed before we're heard, and sometimes we may be viewed and not heard at all. If someone observes you from across the room at a cocktail party but doesn't take the opportunity to engage you in conversation, their sole impression of you from that experience will be based upon what they saw.

Gaining credibility through appearance can be a fickle subject. At first thought, we might assume that in order to gain credibility through the way we look, we ought to look good. That sounds reasonable, and often it's true. To arrive at a typical job interview wearing an oily work shirt and jeans, for instance, wouldn't lend the interviewee much credibility. But if he happened to be interviewing for a mechanic's job, he might have great credibility, probably much more than if he showed up in a coat and tie.

To gain credibility through our appearance, we should consider what's appropriate to the situation. People like people like themselves, so to have credibility in social situations we need to be similar in appearance to those around us. In short, don't wear a tuxedo to the pool hall if you want to be accepted.

The same is true in business scenarios. To inspire the confidence of a customer or counterpart, we must project an image of competence, and that begins with an appearance that's appropriate to our title. An attorney who wore overalls to court, for instance, wouldn't seem too credible.

Speech is the next step in the credibility continuum. After we're judged on appearance, what we say and how we say it will take over in affecting the way we are perceived.

One fall afternoon I went to get grass seed and fertilizer at a garden center where I was approached by an employee who offered her assistance. Because she was employed at a business that specialized in lawn care, and because she was dressed appropriate to the business, I presumed her to be credible. We began discussing overseeding my freshly sodded yard and she recommended using fescue instead of bluegrass, citing disease and drought resistance as the two primary reasons she preferred fescue. She was detailed in her explanation and her words backed up her credible appearance. But when we moved to the subject of fertilizer, I asked her which of the three numbers on every bag indicates nitrogen content, and I was surprised when she hesitated and then rolled a bag over to read the fine print. After a moment she looked up and said, "Yeah, it's the first one." This was a piece of information that I thought any competent lawn care professional should immediately be able to cite, and she couldn't. At that point she lost credibility with me, and not just on the subject of fertilizer. I had to wonder about the accuracy of what she'd told me about grass varieties. To be trusted in what we say, we must be able to affirm our outward appearance of credibility with credible speech.

Actions, though, are the final test of authenticity. There are many people who look the part, a good number who can back it up with words, and fewer who demonstrate it through their actions. What really makes a person credible (or not) is his behavior.

During the time I worked drug cases, I interviewed a number of potential informants. In order to work off charges, get paid, or exact revenge upon an unsuspecting comrade, assorted types were always coming forward to name drug dealers. But names alone weren't much help. We knew the names. We needed people who had enough credibility with dealers to make a controlled buy or introduce an undercover agent. When presented with a prospective informant, we first had to determine what he knew and second, what he was capable of doing with that knowledge.

To judge the credibility an informant might have with a dealer, we had to judge the credibility of the informant. Most of them had curb appeal. They looked the part, a low hurdle, I'll grant you. The second step was hearing what they had to say. Often we knew so much about the identities, relationships, and even specific transactions of those in the drug community that we could measure what a person told us against what was already known. If an individual asserted information that clearly contradicted our intelligence, we suspected he was inaccurately regurgitating what he'd heard, or was improvising to appear more knowledgeable than he was. Either way, his credibility was diminished and we were left with a better understanding of his value (or lack of it) to us.

Sometimes just asking the right question could save a lot of wasted effort. If we were talking about a marijuana dealer, for instance, I might ask the prospective informant, "What's Billy's price?" If he answered, "Fifty bucks," I knew that the person sitting in front of me was buying quarter ounces, a user quantity. An answer of "$1,800.00" would indicate that this person was buying pounds. By listening to the answer of such a simple question I could judge several points at once: whether the potential informant buys to use or buys to re-sell, the quantities the dealer handles, and the degree of credibility the person has with the dealer, given the quantities they're accustomed to exchanging. Occasionally, I heard answers that indicated the person was fabricating or regurgitating information. An answer of "five dollars" to the same question would reveal the person to be a fraud, since that figure doesn't correlate to anything in the marijuana market. Some people will do anything to get out of jail, imperil a foe, or turn a buck, and that includes trying to con a cop.

There were occasions when an informant looked good, sounded good, and then failed to produce when put in the trenches. Since some touted claims that exceeded their capabilities, only with a road test could we be certain of one's worthiness.

I learned a lot about credibility in the years I worked drug cases. It wasn't a college class on credibility, it was a masters course. Formally speaking, it was the first time that I was ever trained on the subject. Informally speaking, I must admit it was the first time I'd ever given the subject of credibility any thought. To that point I had primarily been a uniformed street cop. In that role I didn't have to do much to earn credibility. It came with the patrol car, the uniform, and the badge. Given all the visual trappings, I had credibility so long as I didn't do anything to undermine it.

But working undercover was entirely different. I have said that we all have "presumed credibility." But there's at least one group of people that don't subscribe to that principle—drug dealers. When it comes to selling dope, they don't presume anyone is credible (and therefore trustworthy), particularly people they've just met. Because selling drugs incurs risk that the average person doesn't have to deal with when they meet someone new, a dealer can't afford to presume a new face is credible.

So where did my credibility go, and where would it come from now? As a uniformed cop I had credibility because of who I was, the obvious position I held. Undercover I was just a guy in a worn out t-shirt driving a rusted-out Malibu. I had no foundation for credibility, in fact, I was instantly considered not credible. The first time in, at every apartment or house trailer, I was always a new face that had to be developed into one worthy of trust.

My new credibility would come from informants. If an informant was viewed by a dealer as credible (and therefore trustworthy), that credibility transferred to me. The dealer trusted the informant and the informant was vouching for me: "This guy's a buddy of mine. I've known him a long time—he's all right."

Good or bad, an informant's capabilities were usually evidenced pretty quickly. We could knock on a door, go inside, shake hands, and instantly I would start to get a sense of how much credibility the informant had in the room. This wasn't due to any mystical abilities on my part, it was just that obvious. The real measure of the informant's credibility wasn't gauged by the way he was treated, but by the way that I was treated.

Despite informants with solid credibility in the drug community, there were dealers who couldn't bring themselves to trust a new face no matter who introduced it. An agent I worked with tells the story of such a person who lived in a secluded spot on the edge of the Ozark Hills. Despite several low-key visits to his home, the agent had been unable to make a buy. In fact, the man avoided the subject of drugs altogether.

One afternoon the agent and his informant arrived at the fellow's house where they found him sitting on a picnic table in the back yard. A few minutes into the visit the man pulled a pistol from the small of his back and put it on the table. Though he wasn't threatening them, the gesture was obviously meant to intimidate.

The agent had a decision to make. He had a gun of his own, but drawing it would not have been appropriate. What he did do was spontaneous and natural. He grabbed the pistol from the table, swung around, and fired two shots through the front of an old wood out-building that stood some fifty feet from the house.

It was daring and it worked. Through his actions this agent proved himself to the dealer in a way that mere words never could. The agent did something this man never expected, certainly something he wouldn't expect a cop to do. From that point on he was at ease with the agent, such that the agent would eventually visit regularly without the informant who had introduced them. He also bought pound after pound of marijuana from the man.

We must appreciate that a certain action might lend us credibility in one situation, but strip us of it in another. This agent's tactic worked not because of the act itself, but because of the audience to which he played.

Where Credit Is Due. A close friend once told me, "If you say you're a rebel then you're not one." It's often true: if you have to tell us about your remarkable attributes, they probably don't exist. And if they do exist, your proclamation of them risks the possibility that others won't be inclined to appreciate them. Complimenting oneself is to walk a thin line, and no one can really do it with grace. To get any real credit for talent, honesty, or achievement, we must have the patience to allow someone else to witness those virtues in us. Ironically, we always stand to gain more credit by giving it to others, than by giving it to ourselves.

Be wiser than other people if you can, but do not tell them so.
—Lord Chesterfield

Many people are eager to point out their own accomplishments, but few will point out the accomplishments of another. Still fewer yet have the humility to praise another person publicly for an accomplishment that they themselves had an equal part in achieving. Tabling one's ego and allowing another person to have the spotlight can be difficult. Many find it impossible (or even illogical). But the credibility it will gain the person who does this is substantial. Not only will the credited person recognize the nobility of such an action, others will, too.

It is amazing what you can accomplish if you do not care who gets the credit.

—President Harry S Truman

Though our first instinct is to blow our own horn, an ability to resist this urge and give sincere credit or compliment for what another person has done demonstrates great character.

RAPPORT

After I was promoted to detective, my non-cop acquaintances would razz me about putting suspects under bright lights or beating them with rubber hoses or putting bamboo shoots under their fingernails. And cops are always headed for the doughnut shop, right?

For better or worse, many of our attitudes and stereotypes these days are rooted in what we have seen on television. The image of law enforcement has been molded by this phenomenon perhaps more than any other profession. Maybe that's because there have been so many shows about police. From *Dragnet* to *NYPD Blue*, nothing tops cop shows. Their popularity appears endless. Car chases and shoot-outs are played out dramatically, not realistically. For many Americans, their impressions of the way police conduct business is attached to what they've seen on the screen. When it comes to police interrogations, then, most Americans likely picture a gruff detective, tie loosened and leaning over a small table, yelling at a withdrawn suspect who sits under a bare light bulb. The tough routine.

There have been times when I've thought that real cops have watched too much television. I've seen interrogations in which investigators made statements such as, "Do you know how much time you'll get for this?" and "Are you tough enough to handle yourself in prison?" and "Do you know what they do with punks like you in there?" Did they really expect the guy to say, "Yeah, I've heard the stories, and I'd like to confess now?" Those lines may play well on the screen, but they'll leave you short on results in the interrogation room. You'd never buy a car from a salesman that made fun of your shoes, and you wouldn't confess to a crime after being smacked in the face with all its gritty consequences.

So how does a cop get a confession? Every suspect must be considered individually. The interviewer's approach should be customized to fit the crime, the evidence, and the person. And although there are times when tough talk and figurative threats may be in order, they are the exceptions. Many times getting a confession means choking back the instinctual reaction to someone for the hope of obtaining a greater outcome. Would I tell a suspected thief that I respect him for trying to feed his kids any way he could? Of course. We don't confide in those who judge us; we confide in people who accept us. It's rapport that bridges the gap.

Even a cold-blooded killer like me knows that if you want to touch or influence someone, if you want to change them, you got to get down in their life. You want to change me, rehabilitate me, save me? Okay, you got to understand what makes me tick, what I feel, and why I think like I do.

—Inmate, Leavenworth
Prison; from *The Hot House*,
by Pete Earley

Rapport is born when common ground is struck through positive conversation. If commonalities with another person aren't obvious, they must be found. If conversation fails to come naturally, some improvisation will have to take place. Rapport means being able to relate to someone within their values or interests, something that inevitably establishes good will. Most of us have done this without even thinking every time we've wanted to get to know someone better. Rapport, on a much deeper level, has been at the root of every friendship you've ever had. Its power is indeterminable.

Eye Contact. Because they really are portals to the soul, the eyes can never be neglected in developing rapport. The eyes constantly provide us with insightful feedback on several fronts, the two primary ones being interest and honesty. While the average person may not be astute enough to pick up on the honesty in your eyes, he doesn't need much training to recognize your level of interest in him and what he's saying. Your eye contact will tell him.

Since we typically see people before we speak to them— even if for only a few seconds—the eyes are one of the first barometers of interest. Imagine that you wave to an acquaintance on the other side of a crowded room, and he waves back, then looks away. Wouldn't that give you an immediate sense of his level of interest in you at that moment? You might deduce that he has little interest in speaking with you. What if, on the other hand, that person were to wave back and continue looking in your direction? Wouldn't that give you a more positive feeling about walking over and striking up a conversation? The effect in such a situation would be two-fold. His eye contact (or lack of it) would indicate his interest in you, and that information would then give you the confidence (or lack of it) to walk over and greet him.

Good, natural eye contact is powerful. It makes a person feel he has the listener's attention, that his message is being heard, even if not agreed with. Above all, eye contact—in a cordial conversation—is a sign of respect.

The result of eye contact is determined by situation and usage. Unbroken eye contact in a bar between two men is confrontational. Between the right man and woman, it takes on an entirely different meaning. Good, natural eye contact in a job interview displays confidence and sincerity. While lack of eye contact is usually a sign of disinterest, deception, or even shyness, over the years I've found one situation in which my intentional withholding of it was useful to me.

Only because attorneys have made it so, our criminal courtrooms are awash with gimmicks. Some of them work, some of them don't. Since I was always testifying on behalf of the prosecution, I had it easy on direct examination. The prosecutor would ask me simple and straightforward questions, each designed to illuminate the facts that suited his case.

Then would come the defense attorney. Naturally, the facts that suit the prosecution's case don't suit his client's interests too well. The attorney of the accused would cross-examine me, hoping to redirect or discredit my testimony. A defense attorney, when he can do nothing to legitimately prove his client's innocence, will, among other things, attack the witness. With civilians, they often try confusion. As the renowned F. Lee Bailey has acknowledged, they'll even try leading a witness to adopt quotes he never made. "I like to throw direct quotes at a witness," Bailey once said. "'Did you say this? And I quote...' If he says no, I'll say, 'Do you realize that you said just that on page so-and-so?' He realizes that I've just quoted him directly without having a piece of paper in front of me. After a while, the witness gets frightened. He says, 'I'm not sure.' So I pull out the paper. At the end of the day, if he's a sneaky witness, I might give him a quote that he didn't say, and he'll adopt it: 'Yeah, I think I said that.'"

After a few years of watching attorneys defending their guilty clients with nothing more than smoke and mirrors, I decided to play myself.

I had long understood the accepted role of eye contact in a courtroom. Look at the judge when you speak to him. Look at the eyes in the jury box occasionally when answering the prosecutor's questions. Why? It develops rapport with the jurors and helps assure that the prosecutor's message gets through.

But as my thinking evolved, I came to consider another aspect of my eye contact in the courtroom. If eye contact was enhancing my communication with the judge and jury, was it also enhancing my communication with the defense attorney? Instinctively, I'd always looked at the eyes of a defense attorney when he cross-examined me. Perhaps it was habit, perhaps it was only manners, but just as likely it was my way of demonstrating that I wasn't intimidated. But in doing that, was I inadvertently helping him? Was I allowing him to make a connection with me? Was I actually demonstrating my attention to him, and in so doing allowing him the very respect and comfort I didn't want to provide? I changed my strategy.

If appropriate eye contact promotes good conversation, its absence does the opposite. Imagine trying to make a point with a person who never looks you in the eye. He looks over your shoulder at a distant point. He looks over your head. It's difficult to communicate with someone who denies you eye contact.

I began denying eye contact to defense attorneys as they cross-examined me. My line of sight was always five or ten feet to either side or above their head (enough that they could know I wasn't looking at them, but not so much that the judge or jury realized it). Because I was looking at a wall or faces in the gallery, I had to especially focus on words; an attorney's speech, then, was usually where I noticed the effects of my tactic. As a cross-examination continued, an attorney's argument lost flow. The rhythm of his speech became slightly discordant. Some attorneys were affected by the lack of eye contact more than others, but I'm confident that every one of them sensed something unusual was happening. I am sure many of them didn't realize I was doing something intentional, and there were others, probably, who couldn't put a finger on what was difficult about the cross-examination. There were many times that their questioning was awkward, and I recall at least one occasion on which it was shortened.

I had been testifying about forty-five minutes in a burglary case, using my technique throughout, when the defense attorney asked a rather long-winded question of me, and the prosecuting attorney objected. They both made their arguments to the judge and he said, "Overruled. The officer can answer the question." Still looking over the defense attorney's head, I said, "Could you repeat the question, please?" He stammered for just a moment, said with obvious frustration, "I withdraw the question, your Honor, nothing further," and sat down. His cross-examination was over.

Learning To Listen. The single most powerful tool I've found for building rapport is the ability to listen. There happens to be a dire shortage of people who are willing to simply listen to what someone is saying without interjecting their own experiences and derailing the conversation.

In 1997 I left law enforcement to work in the private sector. I was initially in an office of thirty-plus people where I naturally found myself appraising those around me and how they interacted with one another. I held a position which demanded that I have a good working relationship with everyone, so I thought it best not to get too close to any one person, particularly until I could get a handle on the hierarchy of the office. I stayed neutral, kept to business, and watched with interest.

Soon I realized there were three distinct cliques at work. Though everyone was cordial, it was obvious that members of each respective group didn't spend much time visiting with members of the other groups. Having worked at a police department, none of that surprised me. I knew all about cliques. But after a few weeks, I picked up on something remarkable.

One woman, Rita, was conversing at various times with individual members of all three cliques. Not only was she conversing with them, they were seeking her out. They came to her desk and spoke to her in low voices. More than just niceties were being exchanged—they were confiding in her. Regardless of who had dropped by to visit with Rita, I noticed that the visitor did most of the talking. Rita would give the speaker her full attention and occasionally offer a question or brief remark. She was a good listener and in tremendous demand because of it, to the point that no one cared to which clique she belonged. Because of her broad acceptance, the truth is she probably was the one person in the office that belonged to no clique at all.

In this situation the strategist might want to befriend Rita as well. Being in favorable standing with one member of one clique wouldn't have much weight with people outside of that group, in fact, it would probably simply align you with that clique. But Rita's favorable thoughts of you would travel to members of every clique, and with great credibility, because Rita, largely by way of her willingness to listen, was well liked. Because of that, she had credibility.

When I eventually got to know her well, I nicknamed Rita "The Hub," and I complimented her on her ability to relate to such a variety of people. She seemed a little bewildered by it herself and joked that her frequent visitors could be somewhat of a distraction from her work (a thought she never conveyed to any of them). Rita had no idea what she was doing to make herself a people magnet. It was simply her natural display of interest in what someone else had to say that made her desk a popular pit-stop.

The greatest motivational act one person can do for another is to listen.
—Roy E. Moody

Some of the most popular (and informed) people around are the ones who are content to listen to what someone else has to say. We've all heard people make remarks like, "She talks too much." But have any of us ever heard someone complain, "She pays too much attention to what I say"? Because most people don't recognize this simple skill for what it is, a good listener often gets high marks for being nice, friendly, intelligent, even entertaining—when in actuality they might have said very little. Along with being good manners, listening is a great way to make a connection with someone who has something to say. The world is full of people who love to talk, and if you'll allow them to, they'll love you for it.

The "I" Factor. Now that we've established how popular a good listener can be, understand what the most popular subject of conversation is: oneself. As recruits in the Missouri State Highway Patrol Academy, we weren't allowed to use the words "I," "me," or "my" when speaking to instructors the first eight weeks. The outward reason for this was that the instructors were trying to build a team mentality by eliminating thoughts of individuality. But they were also looking for ways to trip us up, which translated to push-ups, assuming the Cockroach Position, running The Hill, and so on. And what a great technique! Try having a one-minute conversation without saying one of these three words. Why is it difficult? Because we all tend to talk about ourselves. We relate everything to what we have done, what we are planning to do, who we know, and where we've been. "I" is one of the most frequently spoken words in the English language.

Test this the next time you're amongst a group of people in conversation. Sit back and listen how the conversation moves between people. What you'll quickly discover is that the majority of them are talking about themselves. When a new subject comes to the table it will remind another person of something they remember concerning the same topic, and they'll take off like a rocket with their own story: "Oh, I used to...."

Understand this fact and embrace it. Combining the "I Factor" with an ability to listen more attentively can be incredibly valuable. While there are a great many people who love to talk and will need no encouragement to do it, there are those who will be less forthcoming. When conversation is awkward, scant, or non-existent, what does the good listener do then? It's at times like these that we should remember this: everyone enjoys talking about themselves, even the quiet ones.

I never loved another person the way I loved myself.
—Mae West

Asking the reluctant conversationalist about his job or what he does with his spare time often get things moving: "Oh, you collect antique marbles?" or "How did you become interested in marbles?" or "What can some of them be worth?" Questions that allow people to expound on subjects that mean a great deal to them often yield a lot of dialogue and increased rapport.

Even with simple questions, a reluctant conversationalist can be kept moving along. The threshold for rapport is usually crossed along the way and quality conversation takes hold. It could be that it's been quite a while since anyone has given him the stage instead of force feeding their own interests at him. In that case, the problem might become trying to shut the person up. Nevertheless, he'll probably leave with a favorable opinion of the time spent with you, even if he can't quite put his finger on the reason. Of course, you'll know why. You were willing to listen and you combined that with an invitation for him to talk about himself.

You might have heard people talk about having a hard time making conversation in some situation. That's because they tried to do all the talking, and they were right, that's hard work! Making conversation is easy if you simply ask questions of the other person until you hit on something in which he has an interest. Facilitating conversation is so much easier than manufacturing it.

What's In A Name? Years ago a friend used to tease me for using her name continually when we talked. She never mentioned it specifically but would simply smile and stress my name sarcastically when she spoke back to me. I had no strategy in mind by saying her name, in fact, I hadn't even been conscious that I was doing it until she subtly pointed it out. But she was well aware of how often I was saying it. Why did she notice it and I didn't? Because it was her name, not mine. The sound of that word meant more to her than any other in the English language. So it happens to be with all of us.

I'm being realistic, not cynical, when I say that each of us tends to operate in terms of self-interest. This isn't to say that we have no consideration of others, or that we can't see things from another person's point of view, or that we place ourselves above all others at all cost. Rather, we approach life—and especially conversation—in terms of what we have done, what we are planning to do, who we know, and where we have been. I said that our favorite word to speak is "I." Consequently, our favorite word to hear is our own name.

Saying the name of another person is a critical tool in conversation, and there are several ways to make use of it. First, it's a fast and powerful way to build rapport. As a police officer, I often wanted the person I was dealing with to feel at ease with me. Whether it was a witness or a suspect, the bottom line in most situations was that I needed to extract information. Usually, the degree to which people were forthcoming seemed directly proportionate to their level of comfort with me. So how could I instantly increase it? How could I create an immediate sense that they'd known me more than the five minutes they actually had? Leading a person into talking about themselves and their interests is fine in a relaxed social setting, but it wasn't the best route when I found myself standing in a crowded emergency room with an assault victim.

Who calls you by your first name? Strangers? Of course not. Friends do, people that know you, people that you're comfortable with. I realized that to circumvent the Getting-To-Know-You Process and quickly generate that feeling of familiarity, I needed to do something that people close to this person do: call him by his first name. By doing this, I instantly linked myself to the people he's most comfortable with. It works in most any setting. Addressing someone by their first name, appropriately and in moderation, is a great way to lend an instant impression of familiarity to yourself and your conversations.

A second benefit that comes with saying a name is the attention that it immediately demands. Most people will turn their head at the sound of their name more quickly than at the sound of "fire!" Have you ever turned at the sound of your name, only to realize the person was speaking to someone else? The sound of our name is our cue, notice that we're on stage and the point of focus.

If you wanted the attention of a friend on the other side of a crowded room, you might yell, "Hey, Bob!" But what if it's just the two of you? Just because he has no doubt who your words are directed toward doesn't mean you can't (or shouldn't) say his name. When you want a particular point to come through, preface it with your counterpart's name. "I like that idea," doesn't have the same impact as, "Bob, I like that idea." If you get the feeling that you're losing his full attention, insert his name when you speak again.

When two parties are in open disagreement, however, the use of the other person's first name can have a negative feel. If not delivered carefully, "Bob, here's what I'm saying," can sound condescending to the recipient. The situation, our relationship to the other person, and the nature of the conversation must all be considered when we use another person's first name for emphasis.

Have you ever had someone you barely knew greet you by name? If so, do you remember what that felt like? Were you surprised? Alarmed? Flattered? Perhaps it was someone you had a passing introduction to a long while back, forgotten by you if not for this second encounter. It may have been a friend of a friend, a neighbor from the next block over, or someone you met at a seminar months before. Regardless of the particulars, regardless of who says it, the feeling one gets from an encounter like this is something akin to a compliment. We can't help but be pleased that we were memorable enough that someone filed our name away for a period of time and then recalled it so easily. While some appear to have a natural knack for recalling names from distant encounters, most of us have to work at it. It's an admirable trait, and one worth developing.

The Phantom Introduction. Have you ever been introduced to someone, only to find yourself unable to recall their name just minutes later? If so, you aren't alone, and there's good reason for this phenomenon. When we meet another person for the first time, our resources are being drawn upon from several fronts. We need to smile, anticipate the handshake, say our own name, make sensible conversation, consider initiating a well-timed parting, and handle the closing dialogue. Typically, names are among the first words exchanged, at a point where our attention is focused on sizing up the other person and beginning conversation. Though on the outside we may appear cool and collected, internally we're juggling a multitude of mental duties. Unless we make a conscious effort to grab it as it flies past, a name can escape us even seconds after an introduction. When it strikes, we might blame this phenomenon on our bad memory, but the reality is *we failed to listen.*

I used to marvel at those who recall names easily. Probably because I found it difficult, I suspected they possessed innate ability. I was wrong. People who are good at recalling names have simply recognized the importance of them and have worked at listening to, and remembering them. As with anything else that's challenging, the proficiency we get through hard work often takes on the appearance of natural talent.

Just as it gives another person a good feeling when we can recall his name, not being able to will likely leave him with a negative feeling. With that in mind, it's imperative to recognize the importance of names and have a system for remembering them.

First, let's understand where our vulnerability lies. The critical period in remembering a name begins the moment it's spoken and lasts for about the next ten seconds. We have to *listen* first, then take immediate action during this brief window to assure being able to recall a particular name.

The most effective technique for remembering a name

begins with repeating it back instantly. If a man walks up at a gathering and says, "Hi, I'm John Davis," we should respond by simply saying, "Hi, John, it's great to meet you." The primary result of doing this will be that it will help commit the name to memory. If you ever had to remember a quote from a speech or lines for a school play, how did you accomplish that? Chances are you didn't memorize the words by writing them or by thinking of them, but rather by saying the material over and over. The most effective way to memorize words is to speak them.

While we're recording the name in our memory by repeating it, we're initiating something else simultaneously, the initiation of rapport. Why wait for a second meeting to let him hear his name when we can do it immediately?

While working as an undercover agent, it wasn't uncommon for an informant to tell me he had known a target for years, but be unable to give me their full name. Sometimes I was only provided a nickname or a first name. Given that some informants were not too informed and the fact that I could never really be certain whose house we were in, I sometimes found it helpful to pay a visit to the bathroom. With the door locked, I was free to rummage through the medicine cabinet looking at prescription bottles, a pretty good way of getting the true names of the residents.

As a uniformed officer there were citizens that I bumped into on a regular basis, and I don't mean in a negative context. There are many good, pro-police people who enjoy chatting with the local cop when they see him—every time they see him. I carried on with these people whenever our paths happened to cross, in most cases never knowing their names. They were interested in me because I wore a uniform. I was interested in them because that was part of the job, developing rapport with the community we served. On occasion these folks could be great sources of information, too. It was a good proposition for all.

But my street-side politicking had a downside. Occasionally I would find myself taking a report from one of these old friends. Here would be a person I had waved to on a regular basis, stopped to speak with on the street, gone out of my way to say hello to, for years in some cases. After all that time, how could I stand there with my pen and clipboard and say, "Okay, what's your name?" After all, he knows my name, it's pinned right there on my chest. Though we had never been formally introduced, I was sure that these folks presumed that I knew their names as well.

Luckily, I came up with a solution the first time I found myself in this predicament. After covering virtually every other question on the report form—address, date of birth, social security number, the works—I had stalled as long as I could. Then, it came to me. Almost as if it were a mere afterthought I said, "And let me have your *full* name." The inference was that I knew his name, but that I wanted to make sure I had the full legal version for the police report. The technique never failed me, and I have since used variations of it in other situations where I wanted to save someone else's pride and my own embarrassment.

Have you ever been in the position of introducing two people and found yourself unable to recall the name of one of them? Although time seems short when we feel obligated to make an introduction, it's wise to hold back a moment. People with even the slightest degree of social grace have a natural tendency to introduce themselves and will take the initiative if given the chance. It's better they suspect you're unable to recall a name than for you to confirm it by saying, "This is Jerry, and I'm sorry, I forget who you are...."

There will be times when two parties don't make their own introduction, even when faced with a moment of silence. If you feel you have no way out, initiate the introduction and don't be shy. Address the one whose name you can't remember and say something such as, "I'd like you to meet Basil." Speaking directly to the one whose identity escapes you gives the appearance that you're comfortable with him (and his identity). The odds favor that he will then say his own name as the two shake hands. While we worry about appearing silly in situations like these, that fear is largely unwarranted. I've found it virtually impossible to introduce two people without them speaking over me as they say their own names.

The Big Taboo. Clearly, referring to a person by name holds great benefits for all involved—but only if it's the correct one.

When I was ten years old there was a single woman in her fifties that lived in a house behind ours. Though we didn't see too much of Ms. Aslin, my father would occasionally chat with her at the back property line as they both burned their trash in barrels, and occasionally she would summon him for assistance on minor household problems. When a situation arose that exceeded her scope of talent she'd telephone and ask to speak with "Harold."

My parents could never figure out where she had gotten the idea that my father's name was Harold. My mother, especially, always got a real charge out of hearing this, since "Harold" bears absolutely no resemblance to my father's name. They never bothered to correct Ms. Aslin, partly to avoid embarrassing her, and partly, I'm sure, because it was such entertainment to hear her call him Harold. There was, of course, no ill-will over this misnomer, so while it didn't damage their rapport, it certainly overshadowed every other aspect of Ms. Aslin's personality. To this day, the only thing any of us remember about her is that she mistakenly believed my father's name was Harold.

But not all examples of mistaken identity are this humorous. Introduce Richard as "Larry" one time and see how it goes over. Depending on whether a gaff like this is committed in the boardroom or on the patio, one could miss a promotion or simply get slapped on the back and laughed at. It's better to be quiet than to be wrong. If you're not absolutely sure of who you are speaking to or who you are introducing, stay silent. The only thing worse than not being able to recall a name is recalling the wrong one—and then announcing it.

RESPECT

The first two cornerstones of influence—credibility, and rapport—affect how comfortable a person will be with us in conversation. Our own credibility and the degree of rapport we have with a person in a given conversation will determine how much information he gives us, and how accepting he will be of what we give him.

How much we are respected (not to be confused with *liked*) by that person, determines how much confidence he will place in us. The degree of confidence a person has in us is the same degree to which we can influence his thoughts, beliefs, or actions.

The importance of this last cornerstone shouldn't be gauged by the amount written here on the subject. The importance of respect is obvious. Respect isn't developed specifically, it's the result of other factors, like how we conduct ourselves, how we treat others, and what we've achieved. Respect is an end, not a means, and it develops more slowly than either credibility or rapport.

The Right Start

Spatial considerations and physical obstacles are critical in conversation. Can you establish rapport or influence another person standing a hundred feet apart? Over the phone? Through a glass window? Not likely.

While investigating for the defense of a civil suit, I needed to schedule an interview with a man convicted of an armed robbery where he shot a store customer. As I arranged the interview, the legal director at the penitentiary asked if I wanted a face-to-face interview, and I told her that was my preference. Had a contact visit not been granted, I probably wouldn't have bothered to make the trip. I realized there would be enough obstacles in trying to gain the trust of this inmate without having to do it through a partition. Is it easier to hang up the phone on a salesman than slam the door in one's face? It is, because the phone is a buffer. It diminishes the obligation of courtesy we feel when we face someone mere feet away. Whether it's a window, a desk, or a picket fence, physical barriers have the effect of creating distance between people.

While barriers can no doubt hinder communication, we need to appreciate that they can also have a place in the communication process. Pick one of your neighbors and think back to when you first met him or her. How close did you get to them during that first exchange? Maybe you just waved and shouted a greeting. Or it could be that when you both saw that the other was receptive, you moved a little closer and conversation began. Even so, chances are that the two of you didn't stand within arms length of each other during that first encounter. It was a feeling out period in which you were both evaluating one another. In such a situation, an obstacle like a fence between two people might actually facilitate conversation. For someone who's less outgoing, a fence would provide cover, making them feel less exposed and safer in continuing deeper into the exchange.

In some situations it might be wise to actually *create* a barrier. Since a barrier sometimes lends a bit of security to a person that feels hesitant, nervous, or even reluctant to talk, consider standing on the other side of a desk from your counterpart, talking across a car hood, or improvising with whatever happens to be available.

When physical objects aren't available, use space. Distance alone serves as a barrier, increasing the comfort of both parties. Since rapport follows comfort, it should be the first consideration. As a conversation develops and the other person becomes more at ease, consider eliminating the barrier or narrowing the distance.

There's a comfort zone that surrounds all of us. Have you ever had a casual conversation with someone who got within inches of your face when they spoke to you? Do you remember how that made you feel? Threatened? Violated? Offended, maybe. If you've experienced this, you understand what proximity can do to conversation. If that person was trying to build rapport, he probably failed. The rest of us will fail, too, if we don't recognize that speaking distance relates directly to rapport. Generally speaking, people get uncomfortable when these distances are violated:

Intimate:	within two feet
Personal:	two to four feet (familiar parties)
Social:	four to eight feet (introduced, but unfamiliar)
Public:	eight feet and beyond (unfamiliar parties)

It's safe to say that less rapport would be required to interact in the social zone than in the intimate zone. As you found when you dealt with Mr. In-your-face, others must earn their way through our comfort levels. Someone who enters the intimate zone when only qualified for public will likely set himself back in the rapport-building process. When speaking to others, our distance must be consistent with the current level of rapport we have with the other person.

THE WELL-ROUNDED PACKAGE

To be successful at building credibility, rapport, and respect, we must make certain that our physical demeanor is consistent with our words. If we look over someone's shoulder intermittently as we verbalize interest in them, for instance, we'll fail. If we call out to others or say more than "I'll be with you in a minute" to someone else, we'll fail. If we don't stand facing the other person with our arms uncrossed and an interested expression on our face, we'll fail. If you've ever had a salesperson say, "Can I help you?" and a moment later dash off to answer a phone, check out another customer, or go to a back room to help a co-worker with a problem, you know how annoying a lack of sincere attention can be. If your actions fail to back up your words, what you say will seem patronizing and contrived. Rather than build credibility and rapport, you will run the risk of offending that person.

You know darned well that nothing delights us more than being enjoyed, appreciated, or just plain liked by someone, right?
> —Buddy Love, played by Jerry
> Lewis in *The Nutty Professor*

While showing interest in what someone else has to say is mannerly, useful for establishing their baseline responses, and great for developing the three cornerstones of influence detailed in this chapter, it needs to be done naturally. Be patient—don't press too hard or advance too quickly. Above all, be sincere. You may be dealing with someone who's never studied body language or verbal cues, but know that he'll sense it when your interest is not genuine.

Influence And Acceptance

Despite what some say about enjoying a good debate, there's no doubt that people enjoy being in the company of others who share their convictions. Agreement feels good.

In conversation, agreement equates to power. But we know that not every conversation starts off with agreement. Realistically, not every conversation can end with agreement. But having an awareness of both what to avoid and what to seize in conversation will ensure that those which can develop agreement, will.

Argument

To either defend or advance our positions through argument is instinctual. We do it because we've seen it done so often, because we've done it ourselves so often, and because it really is the most effortless way to address someone who rejects or opposes our point of view on something. We can trade sharp come-backs, embarrass the other guy, or pin him into a corner. When we feel as if we're getting the upper hand, there can be great satisfaction to be had, at least for the moment. When someone counters us with words, we naturally tend to fight back in kind.

Though their variations are numerous, there are essentially two modes that guide our roles in arguments—defense and advancement.

DEFENSE

When our beliefs, statements, or proposals are under attack, we invariably find ourselves on the defensive side of an argument. To be in the position of justifying what we've said, done, or advocated can be precarious and uncomfortable.

When someone looks us in the eyes and says, "You're wrong about that," and then proceeds to announce to us (and maybe everyone else within earshot) just how it is, what's our reaction? No one likes to be wrong, and more importantly, no one likes to be *told* he's wrong. If persuasion is the objective of the person doing the telling, he'll fail. Most people have a hard time admitting to themselves that they're in error. Admitting it to another person is out of the question. So can we realistically expect a person to acknowledge they were wrong about a particular point simply because we've out-argued them?

Can you think of a time when you were in the position of defending yourself in an argument? Where was your attention?

Were you considering the other person's points? Did you even have time to? You were probably focused solely on your own point of view and on how to out-maneuver your opponent with your next comeback. While your adversary was trying to convince you he was right, you were focused on how to overcome him.

The very nature of argument demands that we concentrate on our own beliefs, not on those of the other person. Likewise, when we put another person in the defensive position, we are assuring that their mental resources will be allocated to refuting our points rather than considering them.

ADVANCEMENT

If you've ever had an idea shot down by a pessimist, you understand why arguments begin. Our own ideas and beliefs are precious to us. Because they are ours, they are "right." When another person fails to accept what we know to be worthwhile and correct, we feel the need to bring them to our way of thinking. Even if we begin with diplomacy and restraint, often we find ourselves frustrated by the resistance and the situation degenerating into an argument.

When we're on this side of an argument, that is, trying to win someone to our way of thinking, there's a great risk of placing that person in a position similar to the defense mode just described. Though he is only defending *against* our message, the effect can be the same as if he were defending one of his own. Rather than absorbing the good points we bring out, his focus may settle on how to make his next retort and overcome us.

The adversarial nature of the argument always forces each half of the exchange to dwell on his own points rather than those of the other contestant.

If you argue and rankle and contradict, you may achieve a victory some-times; but it will be an empty victory because you will never get your opponent's good will.

—Benjamin Franklin

DEFINING VICTORY

Whoever hopes to "win the argument" should stop to consider what he really hopes to win. Though people ostensibly argue to persuade, that's rarely the outcome. An argument is essentially a contest, and a contest without a score. Victory is usually self-proclaimed, and usually both parties proclaim it. Since these can be clashes of ego as much as of ideas, who wants to concede defeat? When the argument is over, we will still perceive the issue the way we did before, as will our opponent. Though sharp remarks and counterattacks can give one person his sense of victory, they will have made the other dig his heels in, leaving him more convinced than ever he is right.

I have never met anyone who was known because he could argue well, but I have met a few who were well known for arguing.

—S. Lee Ritter

Arguments are useless for influencing others. If you doubt that, consider this: have you ever walked away from an argument and thought anything remotely like, "I lost, and now I agree with them?" If you're like most of us, you'll have a hard time even remembering the argument you lost.

While argument can't be relied upon as a means of influencing the other participant in a conversation, it may sometimes persuade onlookers to our way of thinking. This may be the only situation in which argument results in influence. When we have bystanders present, what would otherwise be a mere argument between two becomes a debate that will be judged by those who happen to be ringside. Since a mere observer has no pride at stake and is not preoccupied in coming up with the next masterstroke, he's more likely to actually digest some of the points that are made.

I argue very well. Ask any of my remaining friends. I can win an argument on any topic, against any opponent. People know this, and steer clear of me at parties. Often, as a sign of their great respect, they don't even invite me.

—Dave Barry

If the purpose is to vent frustration, humiliate, match-wits, or just have fun, then go ahead and argue. But if the goal is to be in a position to truly influence the actions or beliefs of others in a lasting way, avoid argument at all cost. To get what we want, we must be moving in the same direction as our conversational counterpart.

The Alternative

If argument is off the table as a means of persuasion, we must have an alternate way of dealing with those who are adverse to our proposals. It comes through strategy, the thing that few people associate with conversation. The components of a successful approach rely on the institution of control, avoidance of emotional and ego factors, and a focus on advancement rather than defense.

CONTROL

I put control first because it's the bedrock for establishing and maintaining power in conversation. I don't refer to having control over another person or even having control over a conversation, but to having control over *ourself*. If we have that, control in those other areas will follow.

I noted that as cops we knew which of our fellow officers

were apt to get us into a fight on the street. Many of the calls we handled were emotionally charged before we arrived, and an officer's lack of emotional control was sometimes the final ingredient that made a situation overflow. The explanation for why some of these situations exploded is easy to see.

Even someone who has contempt for the law appreciates what a uniformed cop represents. I've heard a lot of people who were charged with serious crimes say to the officer who made the case, "I know you're just doin' your job." Oddly, most bad guys have a peculiar kind of respect for police and their position. When a uniformed officer shows up at a domestic disturbance, he has that appreciation and respect. The officer can be stern. He can even raise his voice or issue commands. But if the officer shows anger, uses profanity, or allows himself to argue with anyone present, he lessens himself. At that moment he gives up the mystique the uniform brought him and he takes on the attributes of an Ordinary Joe. He becomes a person, not a symbol. At best, the situation becomes more difficult than it should have been. At worst, a fight ensues.

People follow emotions. Surely you've seen people lose emotional control because they were dealing with another person who had already lost theirs. It's contagious. People tend to match the emotional tenor of a situation, particularly if they feel threatened by it.

The good news is that *having* control of one's emotions is just as contagious. There's always one person in every conversation that you can control: yourself. If you get excited or angry, others will follow. If you are rational, they will also follow. Our self control, like the police officer's, inspires respect and fosters an air of discipline. With emotion removed from the equation, our points will always have greater clarity and impact.

Funny as it sounds, you get control by having it. It's been my experience time and again, regardless of the situation, that the person who maintains emotional control in conversation ends up with overall superiority in the conversation.

STAY ON ISSUES, NOT PEOPLE

The role of ego in conversation is overwhelming, particularly in ones where differing points of view are held. An insidious problem arises in conversation when we allow our focus to leave the given issue and move to people. Because ego is an ever present force in all of us, sometimes the impetus for this can be very slight.

One way that focus gets shifted from issues to people is when the word "you" is employed in making a point. We make remarks such as, "Are you listening to me?" or "You don't understand what I'm trying to say," or "How can you say that?" Phrases like these move the emphasis off the points we want to get accepted and onto "you" and "me." Worst of all, they agitate the ego. When a person feels he's become part of the issue, his ability to hear our case clearly and objectively will be diminished.

To gain another person's acceptance of our statements, we must stay on the strong points of our case and not allow the focus to drift onto the people discussing it. A person might be persuaded to support an idea other than his own, but asked to support egos, he'll always choose his own.

ASK QUESTIONS THAT MAKE YOUR POINT

It has been said that the shortest distance between two points is a straight line. Though correct, the old saying doesn't mention anything about a straight line being the most prudent course. Particularly when we're passionate or enthusiastic about a belief, we tend to be direct or abrupt with points that we feel support it. While being direct or abrupt may feel natural to the speaker, it won't feel natural to the listener. People don't like being told what to do and it's even more true that they don't like to be told what to think.

Introducing an idea through a question is a great way to gain its acceptance without raising defenses. Questions are less threatening than statements, don't provoke the ego, and give the impression that the recipient had an equal hand in arriving at a conclusion. Since people like their own conclusions better than anyone else's, and resent having another person's thrust upon them, this can be an invaluable approach.

An additional point to consider is that as a general rule, the person asking questions in a conversation is the one in control. This is so because questions dictate the subject and course of conversation, and with more real force (and less apparent force) than do statements. What's more engaging: "Let's talk about football," or "Who's your favorite in the playoffs?" Questions not only determine where a conversation will go, but by design they immediately involve the other person in getting there.

If we can have the humility and patience to allow another person to arrive at our conclusions though their own reasoning, we'll not only get more of our ideas and proposals accepted, but the people who accept them will have more commitment toward them.

DON'T DEFEND YOUR IDEAS

Since conversation is such a fast, fleeting, and unpredictable medium, we should seize upon the few areas that we can control. One of those areas, surprisingly, is whether we're in a position of defense or in a position of advancement. The two positions in argument happen to also be the two positions we can find ourselves in when trying to influence a person through more civil means.

When we want another person to accept our ideas or beliefs, we always want to be on the side of advancement, that is, putting forth the points we want accepted. To the contrary, conversations in which one person tries to influence another typically go wildly off-course and with lightning speed. One party advances a point that supports his case. The other party refutes the point, which places him in the position of advancement—he is advancing a counter-point. The original advancer will then direct his efforts toward addressing the counterpoint, which places him in the position of defense. Not only is he operating from the disadvantaged position, he has allowed himself to be lured into a tit-for-tat debate over a specific—and often inconsequential—counterpoint, while his real case goes untended.

There are several dangers in allowing conversation to erode this way. First, the person who hopes to influence has allowed himself to be put in the defensive seat, the place that is useless for influence. Second, this is the quick way to argument, the death-knell for influence. Third, objections are often phrased in question form, such as, "If that's the case, then why was Northcutt fired?" This is undesirable because the person asking the questions is the one in control of a conversation. If we're trying to gain acceptance of what we have to say, we don't want to afford the other party the power to set the course of conversation through their questions.

Politicians have the reputation of dodging questions, but what they actually do is cling to the position of advancement. Questions dictate the course of conversation, so when a public fig-ure receives a question he doesn't want to field, he redirects the con-versation. Suppose a reporter asks a candidate, "What's your response to your opponent's accusation that you've distorted his record?" The candidate might respond by touching on the cam-paign generally, then moving into his own record, describing his sup-port of farm subsidies, or increased agricultural exports, or increased import tariffs. Of all the ways he might answer, there are two ways that he will not: he will not admit to distorting his oppo-nent's record, and he won't defend himself. Politicians understand that defense is a position of weakness—good ones won't go there, but will instead use the opportunity to champion subjects of their own choosing. In conversation, the best defense is a good offense.

DRAW ON THE RECORD

One way to demonstrate the appeal of an idea or belief is to draw on convention, what others have done in similar cases, or on accepted standards of morality or legality.

Although each of us likes our own conclusions better than another person's, we are also inclined toward going with the pack. Contradictory as this may seem, it isn't at all. We may come to our own conclusions on issues, but those conclusions are often shared by some number of other people. Perhaps it's not so much a matter of wanting to make our own decisions as it is one of not wanting the decision of a specific person cast upon us.

Citing outside references is helpful in giving our proposals weight. It removes us from the equation. We are no longer asking the person to accept what *we* have concluded, but what uninvolved third parties have concluded. This is particularly helpful when we have made the mistake of allowing the conversation to move off an issue and onto people (ourselves), when opposing positions have been taken, or when argument has set in.

By drawing on the record, we allow the other side a way out which does not endorse us, but merely adheres to what is sensible or right in a broader sphere of judgment.

What's In A Personality?

What makes an ironclad criminal case? A great witness? Solid evidence? A victim who can identify the perpetrator? Though many viable cases are absent one or more of these elements, all are undeniably critical. They not only point an investigator to his suspect in the early stages of an investigation, but will later make the case a success in court. But even the investigator who has all of these things still wants to add the crown jewel of any great case, a confession. Regardless of what other evidence might exist—fingerprints, surveillance footage, DNA—there is nothing quite so damning as the accused saying, "I did it."

So what makes one person a better interrogator than another? Why is it that some officers consistently emerge from the room with a signed confession and others consistently manage to provoke the suspect into asking for an attorney? It's usually not the result of mere happenstance. There are a number of abilities that when combined, produce positive interrogation results on a reliable basis.

Certainly near the top of the list is adaptability. The ability to adjust oneself to differing situations, or more importantly, to differing personalities, is a powerful trait to have whether you're in the business of crime fighting or any other.

In his 1921 book *Psychologische Typen*, renowned Swiss psychotherapist Carl Jung wrote, "When we consider the course of human life, we see how the fate of one individual is determined more by the objects of his interest, while in another it is determined more by his own inner self, by the subject. Since we all swerve rather more towards one side or the other, we naturally tend to understand everything in terms of our own type."

In this statement Jung refers to extroverts and introverts, the two most basic categories of human personality. Though these are familiar terms to most people, they're often used flippantly. During the course of conversation someone may remark that "Gerald's introverted," and then move on to other subjects without ever actually making use of this observation or even stopping to consider whether it could be useful.

Adapting to the personality traits of others is a powerful step toward either influencing their beliefs or judging their veracity. A lumberjack can't work without an axe, and no one can get everything that's possible from conversation without being cognizant of personality types and bending to meet them.

Extroverts And Introverts

Though Jung is universally credited with developing the theories of human attitude known as extroversion and introversion, Furneaux Jordan, F.R.C.S., was actually his forerunner in this area. Jordan outlined the characteristics of the extrovert and introvert in both sexes, using descriptions that at times are humorous. The "extroverted woman," Jordan wrote, "...goes even further than Lord Beaconsfield in the belief that unimportant things are not very unimportant and important things are not very important." Jung, commenting on Jordan's observations, remarked that, "This familiar type of woman is extroverted beyond a doubt...the continual criticizing, which is never based on real reflection, is an extroversion of a fleeting impression that has nothing to do with real thinking."

So what are the differences between the two? Although to be termed an introvert may have a negative ring to it (especially to the person the term is applied to), neither classification should be considered better or worse than the other. Extroverts relate to the objective, to that which is around them, to other people, to material things. Introverts relate more to the subjective, to their own impressions, thoughts, and feelings.

Despite that Jordan and Jung defined extroverted and introverted characteristics individually for men and women, the two categories are, for purposes of application, essentially the same regardless of sex. Extroverts are generally more outspoken, quicker to take action, and may be given more to impulse. Introverts tend to be more reserved (particularly in group settings), more emotion-based, and private. Some common characteristics of each type:

Extrovert	Introvert
speaks at a quicker pace	speaks at a slower pace
immodest	modest
out-going	reserved
egocentric	emotion-based
prefers facts over theories	logical thinker
realistic	rational
talkative	good long term memory
impulsive	organized and well planned

None of these traits should be considered mutually exclusive. Certainly an introvert could be outgoing at a social event, or an extrovert could approach a problem rationally.

It's also important to point out that not everyone can be fit strictly into one category or another. While there are some who are extroverted in every way, and others who are introverted just as extremely, many people exhibit features of both types from time to time. Situation, mood, and circumstance affect how a person will behave or think. The point to remember is that people usually lean toward one way more than the other.

Here's where adaptability becomes important. Although we may be dealing with someone we've always considered an extrovert, he may be behaving like an introvert *today*. The same could be true with an introvert who is exhibiting more signs of extroversion than he normally would. Because our goal is to relate to another person at a specific moment, during a specific conversation, we must be able to recognize their *current* mode and be willing to adapt to it. Remember the prophetic words of Carl Jung: "Since we all swerve rather more towards one side or the other, we naturally tend to understand everything in terms of our own type." That type, as you may already understand from experience, can shift in a moment.

Since we "tend to understand everything in terms or our own type," does it seem logical that two people of the same type would relate better? Interestingly, most people go through their days behaving the way that feels most comfortable to themselves, with no consideration of what makes the people they deal with comfortable. We've even heard the boisterous types who proudly proclaim that people can accept them as they are, or else. This is a perfectly fine attitude to have if they don't care what others think of them, if they don't care to have the support of others to accomplish what they want, and if they don't care whether others accept their thoughts and ideas.

I don't suggest that we cater to other people or misrepresent our own personalities. If we're to succeed in conversation, however-er, we must remember that people like people like themselves—when we can relate to someone within their own operating system, we're better positioned to have influence and thus better positioned to detect deception.

Adapting To Personality Types

On a Friday afternoon in the spring of 1992, I happened to be the detective on-call when a homicide was reported. A young man and his girlfriend had brought a two-year-old girl they had been babysitting to a local hospital. At the emergency room the man remarked that he had been bathing the girl in a tub and added, "She just quit breathing." She never regained consciousness and was pronounced dead within an hour of her arrival.

As if this man's odd account of what had happened weren't enough to make one suspect him, the girl had fresh bruises on her forehead and legs, as well as a skin-breaking bite mark on one arm. Perhaps the greatest indication the man might have been responsible for the girl's injuries was the fact that he departed the hospital even before learning of her outcome.

We located the suspect at his home, and he agreed to take a ride to the police department. He was tall, thin, well-mannered and quiet, a man unfamiliar to us and without a criminal history. A fry-cook with reliable work habits at a local steakhouse, he hardly seemed like the type who would beat a toddler to death.

During the evening hours, two of us alternately interrogated the suspect. He looked down during the sessions, spoke softly, and frequently failed to respond to our words.

What he did tell us was scant. He acknowledged being alone with the girl all afternoon. He acknowledged she had wet the bed and that he had spanked her. Those were admissions that helped reinforce the notion of his culpability, but we were far short of a murder confession. After several hours of questioning without any appreciable progress, I decided to change the strategy.

I walked into the interview room carrying the dress the dead child had worn when she was brought into the hospital earlier in the evening. I draped it over the edge of the desk in front of him, then sat down.

My thinking was part right and part wrong. Unfortunately, a little bit of wrong can be hard to overcome in a situation like this one. I was right in my estimation that he was emotionally vulnerable, an introvert. I was wrong, though, in the way that I used that information. What I had yet to learn about introverts who have committed crimes is that they don't deal well with the hard realities of what they've done. The fact that introverts have "thinner skin," so to speak, means not that they will break down under a confrontation like this, but that they will simply *shut* down. That's exactly what this man did. In fact, he didn't speak a word for more than an hour after seeing the dress. For a while there appeared to be little hope of getting any useful information from the suspect, but eventually he gave enough admissions that we were able to have him charged with killing the girl, and months later he pleaded guilty.

My brush with disaster illustrates an important point—recognizing personality types isn't enough. To get positive results in conversation, we must be able to follow that recognition with an appropriate approach.

In another case I worked a few years later, a prisoner in our jail had passed word along that another incarcerated man was making some interesting remarks. A recent burglary of a pizza restaurant had gone unsolved and Kenny was telling a fellow prisoner he was the culprit. He told the other inmate that he was drunk during the break-in and had left his prints throughout the inside of the business. "It's just a matter of time," he told the jailhouse snitch, "until they match those prints to me."

Kenny may have thought his prints were all over the pizza place, but we didn't have any of them. I needed more than the words of a jailhouse rat. I needed a confession, something guys like Kenny don't readily give.

When this situation came along, I was more adept both at gauging personalities and at interrogation. Kenny was a recalcitrant 18-year-old, who even at that age had already managed to put a couple of felony convictions under his belt. He was loud at times, always outspoken, matter-of-fact about everything, and unemotional. He was an extrovert, and I knew they like facts. I would need to prove to Kenny he was caught.

I grabbed a fingerprint kit and went into my lieutenant's office. I pressed my thumb on the chrome trim of his ashtray, dusted the print with powder, then lifted it with tape. I pressed the lifted print onto an index card, then wrote on it the name of the restaurant and the date and case number of the burglary, just as a print from the scene would have been preserved had one been found. Now armed with the hard evidence of his guilt, I had Kenny transferred from the jail to my office.

I read the Miranda warnings to Kenny, and he agreed to talk. I visited with him for several minutes just to open things up between us, then I dropped the index card on the floor between our feet. "We need to get this thing at the pizza place cleared up, Kenny," I said casually. He hung his head, shook it slowly side to side, and said, "I knew this was comin'." Over the course of the next hour, he gave a full confession.

Of course, this confession has to be credited to the good information I had received. Kenny had already convinced himself that his prints must have been found in the burglary scene, so my presentation of "his" print had complete credibility. Had I not been privy to this piece of information, I am certain I could have interrogated him until we both fell asleep. Extroverts aren't easily bluffed, but they will often be truthful when they're presented with facts. It becomes a matter of, "We played, you won, and I'll respect that fact. You got me."

The two personality types approach life with differing emphases and our consideration of those differences will help us connect:

Extroverts
- demonstrate how your proposal benefits them personally
- focus on facts
- appeal to their pride/ego (through flattery or challenge)
- be matter of fact about the issues
- use questions that require "yes" or "no" answers to pin them down
- use realistic language
- rely less on appealing to their emotion
- compliment them, if appropriate to the situation

Introverts
- suggest how your proposal benefits them personally
- appeal to their emotion (and minimize gritty aspects of the issue)
- appeal to their sense of reason
- appeal to their sense of logic
- appeal to their sense of morality
- match their pace of speaking
- match their tone of speaking
- give them enough physical space to be at ease, particularly early on
- compliment them, if appropriate

In both categories I made reference to showing the other party how a proposal benefits them, as well as lending a compliment when appropriate. Because everyone navigates through life with a sense of self-interest and because massaging an ego can lower defenses and build rapport, these are universal.

The Sociopath

While an appreciation of extroverts and introverts alone is empowering in conversation, there is another personality to be aware of, the sociopath. This type really has no direct correlation with the two just detailed, but rather, a sociopath may display mixtures of the characteristics of both. But because his traits more closely resemble those of the extrovert, we should approach him as we would an extrovert.

The mention of sociopaths brings to mind serial killers, and rightly so. In fact, most murderers, serial or singular, are sociopathic. Remorse, empathy, and guilt are emotions they don't possess.

The sociopath does what he pleases, rationalizing and justifying his actions regardless of how horrific they may be. Serial killer Edmund Kemper, who murdered half a dozen women in California in the 1970's, years later justified his spree as the result of his lifelong unfair treatment at the hands of his mother. His discomfort was much relieved when he eventually killed her. Ted Bundy, during a televised interview just hours before his execution, suggested that pornography was responsible for his crimes.

What many may not realize is that sociopaths are all around us. You pass them on the street and stand next to them at the supermarket check-out counter. Nearly always male, most of them go a lifetime without committing any crime, much less murder. Their patterns of behavior, though, resemble some of the underlying traits of the renowned serial killers. They place self-interest above all other considerations and they are masters at rationalizing their actions, the responsibility for which they often attribute to someone else.

Sociopaths crave power, and they can often be found in career positions that fulfill this need. Not surprisingly (or maybe), a large number of those in law enforcement—who undoubtedly hold positions of power—are said to be sociopaths. Some studies have estimated the number to be as high as 20%. About 8% of the general population is thought to fall into this category, and they comprise 40% of the prison inmate population. They commit an estimated 90% of violent crimes.

Curiously, sociopaths are often likeable and seemingly ordinary. While we all share the common traits of self-interest and self-preservation, sociopaths take those tendencies to the extreme, even if at the expense of another person.

The Three Planes Of Navigation

On the path to recognizing deception, we will make use not only of personality type, but other factors as well. We'll need to adapt our approach yet again, but within a somewhat different medium, one I call *the three planes of navigation*.

The Planes

The three planes of navigation have to do with the way we both interpret and communicate with the world around us. They're distillates of the five senses that we've always known: sight, sound, touch, taste, and smell. The first three happen to be the foundations for our "senses" of communication. Some of us relate primarily to what we *see,* some of us relate primarily to what we *hear,* and still others of us relate primarily to what we *feel* emotionally—people tend to be visual, auditory, or kinesthetic.

In conversation, identifying the plane a person is navigating on at a given moment gives us another tool for both depositing and extracting information.

VISUAL

Visual people place greater emphasis on what they see than on what they feel emotionally or hear. This plane contains more people than either of the next two; an estimated sixty percent of the population is visually oriented. Some characteristics associated with the visual person:

- extroverted personality
- talkative
- speaks at a quicker rate
- impulsive, capable of making quick decisions
- inclined to accept positions of leadership

Visual people often use words or phrases that reflect the plane through which they interpret the world:

- "The way I see it..."
- "Do you see what I mean?"
- "Does he get the picture?"
- "I'm still in the dark on this..."

AUDITORY

For those who are auditory, information that comes to them through their ears gets priority. About twenty percent of the population relates primarily to sound, giving them great aptitude for being good conversationalists. This is the most versatile of the three categories. Not only do they generally adapt well to both visual and kinesthetic people, their traits are less rigid than those of the other two groups, which accounts for their flexibility. Some characteristics associated with the auditory person:

- could be either extroverted or introverted
- more reserved than the visual person
- speaks at a moderate rate
- less impulsive; takes time to think before making decisions
- more content to listen to others

Auditory people, too, will use phrases that indicate their mode of interpretation:

- "It just doesn't sound right to me..."
- "That doesn't ring true with me..."
- "She's not in tune with what I've been saying..."

KINESTHETIC

"Kinesthetic" is a seldom used word in the course of everyday speaking, but it's often used in communication circles to refer to the emotional or feeling state. People who are kinesthetic tend to be laid back, show less evidence of stress, and are generally more subdued than either visual or auditory types. About twenty percent of the population falls within this category. Some characteristics associated with the kinesthetic person:

- introverted personality
- reserved, particularly in group settings
- speaks more softly and at a slower rate than either visual or auditory people
- a "thinker," not prone to quick decisions

INFLUENCES ON THE PLANE WE USE...

While individuals lean toward a particular plane, it's important to remember that these are not confining classifications and that we all change planes from time to time. Our ideas, moods, thoughts, memories, fears, wants, and frustrations constantly fluctuate and evolve. Several factors can influence the plane that we "choose" to navigate in a conversation, but the two most powerful are: 1) people present, and 2) topic of conversation.

The people surrounding us often cause us to change to a plane other than our usual one. In social settings, the three planes become a kind of pecking order with visual people at the top, auditory people in the middle, and kinesthetics at the bottom. This ranking is not a reflection of one category's worthiness over another, rather it simply determines who will be the most outspoken, assume a role of leadership, or in some cases even dominate the group. If a visual, an auditory, and a kinesthetic person were engaged in conversation, we could expect the visual person to do the most talking and the kinesthetic to do the least. An auditory person conversing with two kinesthetics could be expected to do most of the talking, or direct the actions of the group.

But what about three kinesthetics in a conversation? Would they just look at one another, none of them stepping forward to take the lead? Likely not, because even when everyone present is reserved or introverted by nature, there will typically be one who is more dominant than the others. The kinesthetic person who assumes that role will take on the attributes of a visual person, though he might never consider being so forward in a group of visual people. Relative to who is present, someone will inevitably move in to take the conversational lead, regardless of their usual inclinations.

The subject of conversation also influences our plane of navigation. People often move from their home plane to one of the other two and back. A kinesthetic person, for instance, might become quite outspoken when conversation moves to a topic he's knowledgeable or passionate about. If you happened to walk into the room at such a moment, their enthusiastic and outspoken delivery might bring you to mistakenly conclude that they are visual by nature.

Just as kinesthetics can move temporarily to other planes, so can visual and auditory people. Everyone goes to the kinesthetic plane from time to time, usually because our own thoughts or the subject of conversation has taken us there. Since the kinesthetic plane is the one that's emotionally based, subjects that evoke personal issues, memories, or sadness, will almost certainly bring the visual or auditory person there. In terms of influencing others, this is the plane-to-plane move that is most significant to us. Of the three, the kinesthetic plane is the one where a person is most workable. There they have the greatest potential to be more open *with* us and *to* us.

Putting The Planes Into Action

Aside from being interesting, paying attention to the planes of navigation can have significant conversational benefits. Since we nearly always accomplish more in our conversations by adapting our approach to fit another person's personality and outlook, we'll need a few tools to help us determine just how that person perceives the world. Our recognition of the planes becomes just that, a tool, and I've found through experience that there are three primary ways we can make the planes of navigation work for us.

MATCH THEIR PLANE TO BUILD RAPPORT

Opposites may attract, but the old saying doesn't say anything about them staying together. People who are different from ourselves may fascinate or captivate us, but ultimately *the people we like most are the people who are most like us.*

Regarding rapport, there are those who will tell you that one of the greatest ways to build it is by mirroring another person's body movements. The idea is that by imitating the body movements of the person you're conversing with, they'll subconsciously think, "This person's like me!"

You know by now that I believe strongly in generating commonalities to create rapport, something this technique is clearly intended to do. And though it sounds plausible, this maneuver has a major shortcoming: our *own* body movements mean virtually nothing to us. Though a trained person can draw meaning from watching body movements, the person *making* them is almost without fail totally unconscious of them. Very few people critique other people's body movements, and virtually no one keeps up with their own. But even more importantly, we place no *value* in our own moment-by-moment body movements. They are not personal to us.

We do, however, place tremendous personal value in our own way of interpreting the world. The planes of navigation are the templates for how each of us will do that. The way we each think, because it is our way, is the one that makes sense to us. We naturally find it both easier and more pleasurable to converse with others who share our way of interpretation. If we cross our arms because we're feeling defensive, that is a gesture produced by external stimuli; there is no internal source for the gesture, so it will create no internal connection with us when the person we're speaking with does the same. Mirroring another person's plane of navigation, though, allows us to connect with a person on a deeper level than is possible through the mere imitation of body movements.

When we determine which plane our conversational partner is navigating in, we can move toward that plane ourselves. If with a visual person, for instance, we might speak at a faster rate of speech than if we were conversing with a kinesthetic. This isn't necessarily a disingenuous move. Everyone moves through each of the planes from time to time, so whatever plane a person is on, we have been there before ourselves. Instead of allowing circumstances to dictate our plane, though, we'll simply choose the one that fits the person we want to connect with.

FOCUS ON THEIR FOCUS

Finding a person's plane of navigation tells us what stimuli mean the most to them. Do they focus primarily on sight, sound, or feeling? Whatever their inclination, we should package our message so that it falls within that focus.

Most people make the mistake of continually packaging their messages according to their own focus, regardless of their counterpart. Of course, the odds dictate that occasionally their focus will match that of the person they're conversing with and the message will get through. But why wait for the odds to pay off?

We can shorten the road to results by packaging what we have to say, sell, or ask so that it clicks. A car salesman who spends his precious moments with a prospective buyer pointing out the great paint job, beautiful upholstery, and sleek contoured styling of the new Brunswick sedan may be missing the mark if he's dealing with an auditory person. While those features would be worth noting, what the salesman thinks is attractive about the car is irrelevant if the prospect doesn't share his priorities. Rather than assuming that the shopper's focus is the same as his own, he should adjust his pitch to match the plane of the person he wants to accept his message. The rich sound of the stereo and the smooth sound of the engine might mean nothing to the salesman, but they might catch the attention of an auditory person.

At the scene of a robbery, or any other crime where multiple witnesses were involved, I often used this concept, but in the opposite direction. Recognizing a person's plane is useful in getting information to them, and it's also useful in getting information *from them*. After conversing briefly with a witness, I could usually determine which plane they were inclined to use, and I adjusted my questions accordingly. Because a visual person relates best to the information he sees, I typically got the best descriptions of cars, weapons, suspects and so on from visually oriented witnesses. Not surprisingly, the auditory people were always flush with details about what was said. Kinesthetics were typically very thorough and were the most reliable witnesses when it came to putting the pieces of an event into sequence. By drawing on the specialties of each group and then combining the information, I always got the most complete account possible of what had happened.

CHANGE THEIR PLANE

Everyone has a primary plane, but situational and emotional variables occasionally cause us to deviate from it to another. Noticing and matching moves between visual and auditory planes can be useful for building rapport or getting a message through, but when it comes to influencing others, it's the move to the kinesthetic plane that we want to watch for. Remember, *"Of the three, the kinesthetic plane is the one where a person is most workable. There they have the greatest potential to be more open with us, and to us."*

Analogies can be drawn between what occurs inside an interrogation room and what occurs in the world outside one, but I can think of at least one philosophical contradiction between those two environments. It's best illustrated by citing a couple of sayings, one you've probably heard, the other you may have not:

Civilians: "You shouldn't kick a man when he's down."
Interrogators: "If you can get 'em crying, keep 'em crying."

The first line sounds noble, but who cares about being noble in a fight? If we really want to win, can we afford to take any option off the table for the sake of being fair? No way.

In reality, the line is used metaphorically, not literally. Rather than an actual physical fight, it refers to an emotional state. When a person is down on his luck, sad, or dejected, we don't want to add to his emotional "defeat." But it represents the notion that when another person is vulnerable, we should give them room.

The cop's philosophy, though, admits what that societal rule of thumb does not. Cops understand that being noble doesn't win fights, metaphorically or literally. When a combatant gets his foe down, an opportunity is presented. Seizing vulnerabilities wins physical fights and it likewise wins conversational struggles. If an interrogator has a suspect to the point of crying, he can't let up. That person's defenses are low and they are as open to being influenced as they'll ever be.

The kinesthetic plane is the one where people are most vulnerable because it is, after all, the plane that is more inclined toward introversion and the one where emotions carry greater weight. Whether a person is usually kinesthetic or just visiting that mode, a person in this plane has lowered defenses. He will give more information and be more accepting of what is given to him.

Though everyone won't be kinesthetic, it is possible to move people to that plane. Because it's the emotionally-based plane, emotions can actually take us there. A person who is visual or auditory may be the most flamboyant and outspoken person on the block, but that same person will immediately go into the kinesthetic plane when he learns that a friend has died. His eyes will drop, his head will lower, and his speech will slow. Circumstances will have taken him against his will to a plane other than his usual one.

There are several techniques that will take a person to the kinesthetic plane. Circumstances will determine which is appropriate to use. As an interrogator, I had great latitude. I could dig up a suspect's dead mother and stand her over his shoulder right there in the room with us and say, "Marvin, you know she'd want you to do the right thing." By bringing up an emotional issue, I would be lowering his defenses and making him more vulnerable to being influenced. Influence in those scenarios meant lulling a person toward giving a confession. Since everyone understands the purpose of an interrogation room, bringing up dead relatives can be fit into the program. Few other settings, of course, will be this forgiving.

One of the best ways to get a person to the kinesthetic plane (or any other) is to go there yourself. By exhibiting some of the attributes of a kinesthetic person, you can actually pull your partner in conversation along with you. We've heard people make remarks like, "He really brings me down," or "I got depressed just being around her." Being around upbeat people brings us up, being around sullen people brings us down. This is why I say that mirroring does work when it comes to planes of navigation; the proof is in the fact that we all do it unconsciously.

Assuming some rapport with the person is developed first, there are several kinesthetic traits that will help in moving a person to that plane. Slowing one's rate of speech and lowering one's voice are two of the most effective. And though preying on their memories of dead relatives won't likely be appropriate, bringing up other solemn subjects might. As soon as it seems natural to do so, get away from chit-chat topics and ice-breakers when you have a message you want to get through. Any subject that causes the person to be serious or introspective stands an excellent chance of getting them to the kinesthetic level. Ask how a close family member is doing. Ask about their children. If the two of you have conversed in the past about a personal problem, ask him how it's coming along now. Move away from impersonal topics like weather and news events and toward personal subjects as the conversation allows. When you're both speaking in low voices on meaningful topics, you have the best opening for getting information or getting it accepted.

As always, keep environment in mind. The chances of artificially moving someone to the kinesthetic plane dwindle dramatically when others are in ear-shot. People are generally less candid when others are near and risk of distraction runs high. Choose an environment that lends itself to the mission, or choose to wait.

Life Is A Classroom

Regardless of where I am or who's talking, I'm always listening to the words of other people. It's a habit that came upon me gradually, one that originated when I first began conducting interrogations. As habits go, it's been a great one. Over the years I've learned more from simply watching, listening to, and evaluating others in ordinary circumstances than I have in all my formal study of interpersonal communication.

You, too, have access to some pretty economical research. As you ingest the words of the people around you, consider them against what you've learned formally. I pay attention not to the subject matter, but to the form and delivery of what people say. While most everyone else is focusing on the topic, I'm evaluating the way it is transmitted. That's where the truth hides.

I often find myself unconsciously noticing a person's plane of navigation. One afternoon while waiting to speak with a business associate who was engaged in a telephone conversation, I heard her say to the person on the other end, "I hear what you're saying, and I can see that happening." I was both struck and amused by the combination of planes she had seemingly invoked with this remark. If anyone had been trying to determine this person's plane strictly by judging the words she used, they might have been left a little confused. Was she auditory or was she visual? Her statement contained elements that alluded to each.

This illustrates why we shouldn't expect to conclusively

judge a person's plane of navigation based upon just one phrase. That visual people tend to use phrases which refer to seeing doesn't mean they have a monopoly on those terms. People are more like clay than stone. Though we each have our own preferences and inclinations, we tend to use words that fit the moment.

This woman was actually visual, and her remark really didn't contradict that fact. She used the phrase, "I hear what you're saying" not because of any auditory tendencies, but because she was talking on the telephone. She wasn't using the phrase figuratively, like an auditory person would, she was using it literally. She really was *hearing* what the person was saying. Now think about the rest of the line, "...and I can see that happening." Could she literally see "that" happening? Of course not. She was speaking figuratively.

If we're going to place value in people's verbal references to the three planes of navigation, it will be worthwhile to note whether they're using the terms literally or figuratively. People who use these references literally are picking words that fit the situation. However, when such references are used figuratively, they are indicators of a person's plane—they are evidence of how that person internally relates to the world around them.

Touch Every Base

There will be times when you won't know the plane of navigation of your listener or listeners. You may have an audience of one and be unable to confidently gauge it. You may have an audience of one thousand, in which case you'll have representatives of all three categories. Whichever the case, it's often a good idea to include references to all three planes, particularly when addressing groups of people. By touching on all of the three planes, you'll be more likely to touch every listener.

The Eyes Have It

On a cool Sunday morning in 1989, The King Black Joker hailed me as I drove my cruiser slowly down a west-side street. Sunday mornings are slow for cops most anywhere, and this one was no exception. The Joker, pushing his shopping cart, was the only thing stirring.

The King Black Joker was a shoe-shine man by trade. To those unfamiliar with him, he probably appeared homeless, but that wasn't at all the case. He had a small house from which he ventured early every morning under his trademark straw hat. Packed with assorted unidentifiable supplies, including a guitar he called Troubles, the shopping cart bore a large hand-painted wood sign on the front that identified the man pushing it. The Joker claimed to have shined shoes coast-to-coast. Manhattan. New Orleans.

Phoenix. San Francisco. By comparison, it seemed, he was out to pasture now. Daily, he roamed the streets of our town, rolling cigarettes from the pack of Bugler tobacco that peeked out of his shirt pocket and doing more talking, I suspected, than shoe-shining.

His concern on this day wasn't shoe-shine, or even the Blues records he used to review for me. Days earlier a woman had been found dead in a baseball dugout at a park several blocks from where The Joker found me. "That woman over there," he said with that wild-eyed grin of his, "I know how you can find the person' killed 'er."

I was always fascinated when I spoke with The Joker, but his introduction this time especially grabbed my attention. It wasn't that I expected to solve a murder this morning, but I was instantly captivated by his proclamation. I couldn't imagine what he had in mind. I was all ears.

"You tell 'em to take that woman's eyes out," he said, "and you tell 'em to shine a light through those eyes onto da wall. Right there, just like a picture, you'll see his face on the wall...the last thing she seen befo' he killed 'er."

He had obvious confidence in the procedure's ability to produce a portrait of the woman's killer, and not being one to crush ingenuity, I entertained the idea with him. Being a man of the moment, though, he must have forgotten the idea in pretty short order. On subsequent encounters with The Joker, I always prepared to explain why we had not tried his technique, but it was a subject he never revisited.

The Joker knew the eyes were significant, but he missed the mark on two points. The eyes, so far as anyone knows, don't record anything, and what information they do provide can be found only in the living.

The eyes, it has been said, are windows to the soul. Shifty eyes. Bedroom eyes. Cold eyes. Sad eyes. Amazingly, the eyes are at the same time exits and entrances for information. When we want to make a point, when we're interested in another person or their words, even when we want to intimidate, we look at the eyes. When a parent admonishes, "Look at me when I speak to you," where do the child's eyes go? To the parent's eyes, of course. The eyes are the point of contact. *They are the person.*

In terms of detecting deception, the eyes are incredibly valuable. The foremost reason is that they do transmit information so well. They're full of activity. They move in all directions. They blink. They tear. Additionally, the accepted courtesy of normal eye contact gives us the opportunity to appraise them without generating suspicion or resentment.

Though everyone, knowingly or not, makes use of the eyes in communicating with those around them, there's a definite lack of appreciation for what the eyes can and cannot tell us. Though few are as creative as The Joker's, misconceptions abound. One of the greatest is that breaking of eye contact always indicates deception. I occasionally heard people who were trying to be helpful to an investigation tell us, "I knew he was lying—every time I asked him something he'd look away." Then there were occasions when people would say, "I knew he was lying—he was trying to look honest, he wouldn't take his eyes off mine." You look away, you're a liar. You don't look away, you're a liar. How could anyone win this game!

Contrary to such notions, there are reasons other than deception for a break in eye contact. Manners are one. Continual eye contact is considered rude and people often look away from time to time so as to avoid making themselves, or the person they're speaking to, uncomfortable. It's also perfectly natural—and very common—for a truthful person to look away from one who has just asked him a question. This can occur both when he answers questions as well as when he prepares to make a statement, without regard to his degree of truthfulness. The more memory or thought that's required in putting an answer or statement together, the more likely it will be that the person will look away while preparing it.

Recollection And Construction

In developing an answer or a statement, people draw on two distinct sources: 1) they recall facts from memory, and 2) they construct new thoughts.

RECOLLECTION

Consider your memory to be like a file cabinet. In your file cabinet you have drawers, and in the drawers you have dividers that have individual files between them. Each file contains a specific memory. Some are complete and orderly, others are vague and jumbled, and still others exist, but are not easily accessed. Have you ever had a conversation in which someone brought up an event long passed that you had entirely forgotten? It can be a strange sensation to suddenly have vivid memories of an event that you hadn't thought of in years and might have never recalled again had it not been for a nudge from someone else. The file had been there all the time, perfectly preserved, but for some reason you had been skipping over it.

Your files run the gamut. Some relate to your personal experiences, events that can be as old as your first day of school or as recent as what you ate at your last meal. Other files in your cabinet relate to facts that you've not lived personally, but have only been informed of. You know that Abraham Lincoln was a United States President not through personal experience, but through the experience of learning it from other sources. Whether the information came through personal experience or through learning of another's experience, everything in your memory is historical.

Suppose someone asks Bert, "What president authorized the

dropping of atom bombs on Japan?" Assuming he knows the answer, Bert will pull it from one of his files. Further, if Bert is like most people, he will have to give this at least a moment's thought, so we could expect him to break eye contact as he considers the question and digs for an answer. This would not indicate deception, it would merely be a sign that he needs some room, that he is sorting through his files. When he comes upon the answer, his eyes would probably come back to those of the person who asked the question and he would say, "Harry Truman."

While it may be true that many people place the wrong meaning in another person's breaking eye contact with them, they are right in thinking it has meaning. But not knowing the correct meanings of eye movements, or putting faith in erroneous ones, really renders the eyes useless as tools for communication.

The simple fact that another person has broken eye contact tells us very little. It's the direction the eyes go—either left or right—after breaking that begins to reveal something useful.

To understand what it means when we see a person's eyes break left or break right, we first need to understand a few facts about the human brain. The brain in your head can actually be considered two brains, the left side being one and the right being the other. They are separate in the sense that each side of the brain has its own distinct duties, specialties, and ways of relating:

Left	Right
sound	sight
abstract thinking	factual thinking
rational decision making	impulsive decision making
practicality	creativity
logic	intuition
views things sequentially	views things randomly
views piece by piece	views as a whole

Ideally, the two hemispheres of our brains compliment one another in dealing with information and problems, resulting in a balanced outcome. While both sides are used to varying degrees, people tend to be either "left-brained" or "right-brained." This means that one side, with its associated characteristics, tends to take precedence over the characteristics of the other side.

This isn't to say that a left-brained person lacks creativity, or that one who is right-brained would be unable to make rational decisions. As we find with most other aspects of human behavior, there is a constant give and take, an ebb and flow; we can speak categorically in predicting behavior, but we will be less accurate when we try to predict it specifically or say that it is so in every instance. Nevertheless, we can be confident that a person who is left-brained will generally approach life with different emphases than will the person who is right-brained.

This explains, physiologically, why some people look to their left when they recall from memory and others look to their right. Since the brain is cross-wired so that the right side controls left aspects and vice-versa, left-brained people look right as they go to recollection and right-brained people look left.

The fact that one side of our brain tends to be more influential than the other also relates to extroverts and introverts, as discussed in Chapter 5. Some of the characteristics that describe left-brained people bear resemblance to the traits of introverts and some of the right-brained characteristics bear resemblance to those of extroverts. This represents another interesting and revealing aspect of watching the direction a person's eyes break when he looks away to recall a memory. We'll find that people who look right for recollection tend toward introversion, and people who look left for recollection tend to be extroverted.

We can deduce a lot about a person simply by watching the direction his eyes break when he is recalling from memory. But when it comes to recognizing deception, we need to add another component, the second source that people draw upon when they are developing a statement or developing an answer to a question.

CONSTRUCTION

If you need a loaf of bread, you can either go to a store and buy one or bake one yourself. When it comes to expressing ourselves with words, our options are pretty much the same. Through our abilities of recollection, we can pull an existing piece of information from one of our files, or we can construct something new.

Construction, then, is the opposite of recollection. When Bert was asked to name the president who authorized the dropping of atom bombs on Japan, he used recollection to tell us that it was Harry Truman. The answer to the question already existed, he only needed to find it. What if, on the other hand, we asked Bert, "Do you think the atom bomb could be used again without starting another world war?" Unlike the first question, this one doesn't have a concrete answer. He's not being asked about something that has already happened; he's being asked about something hypothetical, something he'll have to imagine. Try as he might, Bert will never find the answer to this one in his file cabinet. He'll have to *construct* it.

So how does construction relate to deception and lying? From this example, it's evident there is nothing illegitimate about construction per se. We all rely on it every time we have to generate original thoughts or answers and turn them into speech. Honest people use construction everyday, just as Bert would to answer the "Do you think..." question.

But in the case of deception, and especially lying, upon which of the two sources does the deceptive person draw, recollection or construction? Let's consider that. If they were drawing on recollection, they would be recalling fact. Fact is truthful. To the contrary, lies are not factual. Though deceptive statements may contain truthful elements, they are designed to mislead. Just as a truthful person goes there to imagine a hypothetical scenario and then make a statement about it, the deceptive person goes to construction when fabricating a lie or considering an act of deception.

Just as people break eye contact when drawing on recollection, they break eye contact when drawing on construction. The eyes generally break one direction when a person goes into recollection and break the *opposite* direction when he goes into construction.

Again, the fact that the eyes break contact when a person goes to either recollection or construction is not in itself an indicator of honesty. It's our ability to contrast the two that allows us to evaluate deception.

Using Recollection And Construction To Recognize Deception

The majority of conversations require us to alternately use recollection and construction. As we put our thoughts together into words, our minds bounce between recollection and construction. We recall information from files, construct and relate new thoughts, and continually cross-check what we're constructing against what we're recalling.

This cross-checking happens quickly and frequently. If Maxine were asked, "What did you think of Lucy's behavior last night?" we could expect her eyes to go one direction as she used recollection to bring up the memory of what Lucy did last night, then go the opposite direction as she used construction to build her statement. The mere fact that she goes into construction does not mean Maxine is about to be deceptive. Although Lucy's behavior is historical in nature, Maxine's opinion of it is not. It would be perfectly natural for Maxine to move into construction as she transforms her thoughts into words.

How, then, can the recollection/construction phenomenon be used to judge truthfulness? The first step is establishing a baseline for the person to be evaluated. We need to determine how they look and react when truthful.

I would wager that you've already established behavioral baselines for everyone you know well. Through interaction, we come to expect an individual to behave in certain ways. You may have heard someone make a remark such as, "Carl's not himself today." The person who said it saw a person deviating from his normal attitude. Had that been the first day they'd met him, they might have concluded he had an unpleasant disposition. But because they knew from experience how that individual routinely acted and had unconsciously registered his baseline behavior, they easily recognized his aberrance from it and it told them that something was amiss with him. Over time, we come to realize how the individuals around us typically act. Changes in those baseline behaviors tip us off to trouble.

Baselines help in judging eye movements as well. The good news is that unlike behavioral baselines, which are developed over time, we can determine a baseline for eye movement in pretty short order, usually within minutes of beginning a conversation.

In order for eye movements to be reliable, several points should be kept in mind. First, you need to be in front of and facing your partner in conversation. When I refer to a person's eyes breaking left or right, this means breaking to *their* left or right from center. If you're at an angle to the person you're conversing with or to their side, not only will it be difficult for you to see their eye movements well, but the movements won't be of much value. Your positioning will demand that they look to one side just to address you. It's important that you be centered in front of the person you converse with, so that they have the latitude to truly break left or right as they speak with you. In most scenarios, this is easy to accomplish.

Normal conversational etiquette allows us to position ourselves so that we face another person as we converse with them.

Environment is another consideration. Distractions that draw the eyes away can distort results significantly. If you're trying to speak with a person while others are doing interesting things over your shoulder or off to the side, your conversational counterpart may not be breaking eye contact to recall or construct, he may just be curious to see what's happening. Sights and sounds that lure the eyes away make the job of discerning breaks more difficult. The person may go one direction for both recollection and construction, or shuffle the two up in ways he otherwise wouldn't.

Also be aware of physical conditions within your environment. If the person is sitting or standing with a shoulder against a wall, for instance, he probably won't look in the direction of the wall much. People break eye contact because they "need room" to think. A wall or other obstacle that's just inches away doesn't allow that room, and so the person may actually be inclined to break eye contact in only one direction, away from the obstacle, regardless of whether he is headed for recollection or construction.

For these reasons, it's always best to converse in the cleanest environment possible. If distractions or obstacles exist, maneuver into better surroundings or wait until conditions have improved. Police interrogation rooms have nothing on the walls, no windows, and no props to occupy the hands of the person to be questioned. Subjects are seated in simple, armless chairs, away from walls and desks. Though our routine conversations don't occur in such sterile environments, reducing the number of distractions and physical obstacles will increase the odds we'll see meaningful eye breaks.

When properly positioned in front of another person in the best environment possible, we're ready to begin establishing a baseline for their eye movements. In order to recognize deception, we first need to be able to recognize truth, and that means determining the direction a person's eyes go for recollection.

Just like successful police interrogations, successful conversations begin with the development of rapport. When I conducted interviews and interrogations as a police detective, the initial period was non-accusatory and relatively relaxed. My objective was not only to build credibility and rapport with the person during these first minutes but also to determine the direction their eyes went for recollection.

Since information we pull from our files in recollection is factual—and therefore truthful—asking questions that elicit answers we expect to be truthful will tell us the direction a person's eyes go for recollection and thus establish their baseline.

At the onset of an interrogation, an officer can ask a person his date of birth, his social security number, what his mother's maiden name was, how long it has been since he's eaten pizza, or any other questions that a person would have no reason to lie about. But to get meaningful breaks in eye contact, we have to be certain that the questions require a little thought. Personal facts, like one's date of birth, may be so easily recalled that no break in eye contact occurs. I've often found that in order to cause a person to break eye contact and go to recollection, I had to graduate into subjects that the person wasn't in the habit of instantly recalling. If asked, "Tell me what you remember about first grade," the odds favor that the average person would go to their "file cabinet."

Two subjects that people can't resist talking about are where they've been and what they've done, both of which are historical (and hopefully truthful). It's common to hear people recounting their experiences to others, and it's almost always unsolicited. When they do this, they're using recollection. Sometimes they'll actually signal that they're using recollection with remarks like, "I'm trying to think of it," or "I wish I could remember." Notice the direction in which their eyes have broken when you hear lines like these. The person speaking them is using recollection.

Conversely, people often signal that they're going to construction. Introductions like, "Let's suppose...," and "What if...," are tip-offs that the speaker is going to manufacture a statement rather than simply retrieve information. Lead-ins like these are worth noticing not because they indicate deception but because they identify the direction that person's eyes break for construction. Watch the eyes when phrases like these are used. They introduce hypothetical statements, which are products of construction.

In determining whether a person goes left or right for recollection, the conclusion should be based on as many breaks in eye contact as possible. More data always means more reliable results. Watch for a preponderance of eye movement, not a totality of it. A person who looks right for recollection may go left occasionally and still essentially be using recollection. We should notice the direction the eyes go *most* of the time, understanding that people are not machines. The eyes will often wander, particularly in periods of extended contemplation. There's no substitute for patience and practice. Expect to spend a lot of time observing eye breaks before being able to make reliable conclusions.

Let's suppose that after watching the eyes of another person for half an hour you conclude that his eyes break (to his) left when he goes to recollection. Left, then, is the baseline. That is the direction we can expect his eyes to break when he needs to pull information from his file cabinet. When his eyes break the opposite direction, to the right, we can expect that he is moving into construction.

Remember that construction is where one goes to create ideas or statements and that they may be either truthful or deceptive. One might wonder, if construction can be used to produce truthful statements, how then do we know when a person is using construction to be deceptive?

Use the subject matter as a guide. Particularly when posing questions, always ask yourself, "Where should he be going to find the answer: to recollection or to construction?" Questions that regard past events are typically the ones that require the answering person to move into recollection. If you asked Larry, "Where did you eat Saturday night?" you would expect his eyes to break in the direction of recollection, since there is a factual answer to be found in one of his memory files. If, on the other hand, his eyes were to break contact and move toward construction, that would indicate he is creating an answer (and thus being deceptive). Notice where a person goes to get their information, then consider whether that was the logical place to go for a truthful answer.

While in the midst of a federal drug conspiracy investigation in 1995, I discovered another interesting use of eye movement. I was interviewing a man who was part of an expansive methamphetamine network, and because I was already nearly a year into the investigation and had interviewed dozens of the key players involved, I knew much of what this man had to tell me before we met. I was hoping that he would fill in some bits of missing information, corroborate what I already had, and of course, further implicate himself.

A baseline for this fellow's eye movements was easily established. He distinctly and dependably broke eye contact to his left for recollection. Since I was developing a historical conspiracy, what interested me was past information. I wanted names, dates, places, and quantities. Since the information I wanted to hear was in his file cabinet, I expected him to look left when searching for truthful answers to my questions.

Occasionally during our conversation he would look right—his direction for construction—when thinking about an answer. He usually stayed there only momentarily, then went left again into recollection before speaking. Either his eyes were simply wandering about as he thought, or he was considering deceptive answers and choosing not to use them. Since I had the luxury of knowing much of what he was telling me, I could measure his honesty. Despite those intermittent glances toward construction, I felt that he was being truthful.

As our visit progressed, though, I saw his eyes wandering toward construction more. Then I asked a question that concerned how much methamphetamine he'd received one afternoon at a motel. His eyes went to construction, and they stayed there. He was thinking. *He was constructing an answer.* I didn't want him in construction, I wanted him in recollection. Impulsively, I said, "Think back."

I was amazed at what I saw next. His eyes moved away from construction and back to his left, to recollection. "A pound and a half," he said slowly. It was eery! He was about to give me a fabricated answer and I had actually commanded him to get out of construction and go back to recollection, where the only answer he could find was the truthful one. I've since used this simple technique on many occasions, formal and otherwise. When we want truthful answers to historical questions, we want answers that come from recollection. When someone's eyes break in the direction of construction and the answer should be found in recollection, try directing them there. Phrases like, "try to remember," and "think back," actually direct a person to go to their file cabinet for an answer. Often, they will do as they're told.

A former federal agent told me how he made use of eye movements. When he saw an interviewee heading for construction, he would interrupt him and say, "Now, hold it—don't tell me any lies." Some of the people he interviewed wondered if he could be reading their minds! They were astounded that each time they considered conjuring up a deceptive remark, he pointed it out. They had no idea they were telegraphing their thought processes to him.

He was simply watching their eyes as they headed for the construction zone.

In the earlier example where Maxine was asked about Lucy's behavior, I noted that Maxine's break toward construction wouldn't necessarily be an indicator of deception. Unlike a question about a historical fact, the question, "What did you think of Lucy's behavior last night?" inherently demands that she use construction in answering it. When a person has legitimate reason to use construction, we must rely more heavily on other techniques to judge deception, such as verbal and physical symptoms. Watching hand and body gestures, facial expressions, and even noticing the promptness of her answer would help in determining the veracity of Maxine's words.

There is one exception to all of this, the memorized lie. In instances where a person has memorized a lie concerning a past event, he may look in the direction of recollection not to recall facts of the event, but to recall the lie. This happens, but rarely.

Using Eye Movements To Determine Their Plane

Aside from giving us indications of a person's truthfulness, the eyes can reliably tell us whether a person is visual, auditory, or kinesthetic. The eyes are capable of moving more directions that just left or right. When they break contact toward recollection or construction, the eyes also move on a vertical plane: upward, to the side, or downward.

While one individual may break eye contact for recollection and construction in the opposite direction of another person, the eyes are constant when it comes to indicating planes of navigation. Visual people look upward, auditory people look laterally, and kinesthetic people look downward when preparing their statements or answers. Depending upon whether a statement draws on recollection or construction, the person will also be breaking left or right in conjunction with the upward, lateral, or downward break.

One caveat to remember: subject moves people through the planes. If bringing up an emotional subject can draw a person to the kinesthetic state, asking them to describe the sound of something can draw them to the auditory state. A person describing the appearance of a painting, for instance, could be expected to look upward to their recollection side as they recalled this visual information. Making note of the speaker's subject will assure that we don't classify a kinesthetic person as visual, simply because he happened to be accessing visual information.

When it comes to determining which of the three planes a person is operating in, I've found the eyes to be more reliable indicators than verbal references. Although a person who says, "I just don't see it your way," may indeed be visual, there's nothing to keep a kinesthetic person from using that kind of phraseology. Just because visual people are inclined toward those kinds of words doesn't mean auditory or kinesthetic people have an aversion to them. For verbal references to have weight, they need to be multiple or accompanied by other indicators. This is less true with eye movements.

One reason the eyes are so much more reliable for determining planes is that their movements are so fast and frequent. Verbal references may come few and far between, but in one minute of conversation the eyes might break in a direction that indicates plane of navigation a dozen times. I always emphasize the need to evaluate chunks of signs, not slivers. Because they are so full of activity, the eyes provide chunks of data quickly and that makes their information more reliable.

Part III

Tone, Taste, Tenacity

How Do You Say It And Why Does It Matter?

As we go about the task of interpreting symptoms of deception, we'll find that the situations in which we'll need to use these skills will be as varied as the people we evaluate. Still, there are only two basic vantage points from which we will operate. Sometimes we'll be able to interact with the person we're evaluating, sometimes we won't.

We are either participants or observers of conversation. One is definitely preferable over the other. Viewing a politician on television, for instance, affords us no opportunity to ask questions or direct the conversation. We can be similarly handicapped at a social gathering where we may be listening to, more than participating in, the conversation of the person we're curious about.

Involvement is power. It enables us to influence the direction of conversation. When something catches our interest, we can offer questions that delve a little further. We can revisit points that made the person react out of their norm. We can adjust or change subject matter. Knowing the right questions to deliver and just as importantly, using the right delivery, brings the power of involvement to its full potential.

Champion fishermen say there are only three things to remember on the water: presentation, presentation, and presentation. The way we phrase ourselves is our presentation. Every time your mouth opens to speak, presentation plays a greater role in the way your message is received than do the words themselves.

In The Beginning

Never begin a conversation with your main objective. There is a well known credo that when counseling subordinates, good supervisors always start and end with positive subjects, sandwiching any critical or negative subjects in the middle. It's simple advice that makes great sense for a couple of reasons.

When we turn someone off at the outset of conversation, we dramatically reduce our ability to put information into or get information out of the person we're conversing with. Criticism, cute opening quips, and the mention of embarrassing subjects or past conduct can make people defensive. This seems obvious, but it's truly amazing how often people make remarks in the initial stages of conversation that make the other party uncomfortable, defensive, or angry. When this happens, doors close.

Starting off with something positive can have the opposite effect. If we want someone to accept what we have to say, we should first get them in an accepting frame of mind. Great salesmen depend on this technique. They ask series of questions to which the prospect will most likely answer "yes." "Would you like to make more money?" "Would you like your office to be more efficient?" "Would you be open to new ways of increasing employee loyalty?" Questions like these not only get a person into a positive and accepting frame of mind, they actually lead him to practice for the ultimate yes that the salesman is aiming for: "Yes, I'll buy."

This is a technique that applies just as well to conversations outside the sales arena. Beginning with statements the other party is likely to accept, such as, "Would you be willing to give your opinion on another way of doing this?" positions us to gain acceptance of any less attractive items that follow.

First impressions are important, but the last impression is the one that lingers longest, particularly if it's a bad one. To make sure important points stick, end a conversation on the positive side, just as it was started. If an otherwise good conversation turns sour in its final moments, it will be remembered as a bad one. Additionally, any progresses that were made will likely be forgotten.

Two Approaches You Can't Do Without

A business associate of mine who's a former cop has a favorite line that he used on suspects in his past career. He used to tell them, "I don't want a confession; I just want to know why you did it." It's a phenomenal line. It clicks with me because it embodies what I've long considered to be the two most powerful components to have in my approach when I want honest information from another person in absolutely any setting:

1) Minimize your true objective
2) Come from a position of knowledge

My colleague's statement is made of two parts: "I don't

want a confession," and "I just want to know why you did it." With a bit of examination, we can easily see what makes his line so powerful.

MINIMIZE YOUR TRUE OBJECTIVE

Was it true that he, a police officer, really was not interested in a confession? No! Of course he wanted a confession, and even the dumbest of suspects knew it at the outset of their conversation with him.

When my friend told a suspect "I don't want a confession," he was taking the focus of what the suspect was most apprehensive about (questions about whether he had committed a crime) and shifting it to something far less threatening, the seemingly innocuous question of *why*.

Whether our conversation is in the context of a police interrogation, a business meeting, or a disagreement with our spouse, confronting the issue sometimes has a way of disarming our counterpart. Both parties typically know what the points of contention are. When we speak them, the apprehension is often diluted instantly. It's typically the subjects that people avoid talking about that lead us to suspicion their motives. Demonstrate that you have no fear of speaking about a particular subject, and it will demonstrate that you have no dark agendas that relate to it.

Mentioning the negative or threatening issue only becomes a risk when we allow it to become the focus of conversation, so it's important that we don't allow that to happen. If we want to minimize the subject, we have to touch on it and *keep moving*. Mention the true objective as if it were of little interest, then immediately shift attention to a less threatening issue and present that as the important one. When conversation finally comes back around to your true objective, it will likely be much easier to discuss.

Crooks are masters at minimizing their culpability, and it has landed a lot of them in prison as the story of my old friend Roosevelt illustrates. Just after midnight, one of our officers drove down a street that was a popular hangout for thugs and dope dealers. As his patrol car rounded the corner, he saw Roosevelt drop an object and walk away suddenly. The officer stopped his cruiser at the curb and went to where Roosevelt had been standing. In the wet grass he found a pistol. Several hours later and several blocks away he caught up with Roosevelt and arrested him. Like any convicted felon, Roosevelt could not lawfully possess a firearm.

We often pulled people out of jail to interview them, not only to talk about what they had done, but oftentimes more importantly, about what others had done. A great many of our cases were cleared through information obtained from people like Roosevelt. Knowing that Roosevelt was immersed in the criminal street scene, I thought he might do us both some good, so I brought him to my office for a talk.

One would assume that Roosevelt's issue of great hesitation would be the gun, so I began our conversation by talking about other subjects. But as I tried to talk about how he might help his situation, the only thing Roosevelt could talk about was the gun. He continually interrupted to explain the circumstances that led to his arrest, his assertion being that he had been strolling along innocently when he saw a gun lying in the grass, whereupon he had merely picked it up to take a closer look. I wasn't the only one trying to minimize something.

After ten minutes of his ranting, I said, "Look, I know you're upset about this whole thing. I've got a lot to do this morning, but if you have an explanation for how this gun came to be in your hand, I'll stop everything and take a statement from you. You can tell your side of this, and we'll send it to the prosecutor." He was elated.

I proceeded to type his statement and when I finished, he signed it for me. I had Roosevelt's authorized account in black and white. In it he explained that he had been the victim of bad timing. The gun had been in his hand for mere seconds when a police car rounded the corner. Startled at the sight of a cop, he dropped the gun. He had explained everything.

Roosevelt hadn't given an explanation, he'd given a confession. A convicted armed robber and three time felon, he pleaded not guilty, was convicted at trial, and sentenced to more than 200 months in federal prison.

Would I have gotten a confession if I had questioned him directly about the gun? I can't be sure. But it's likely that my interest in the gun would have caused him to realize what a threat it posed and he wouldn't have been so eager to discuss it.

Bringing attention to and then immediately shifting away from the true objective has great potential. Sometimes you won't even need to revisit it. As Roosevelt's tale demonstrates, they just might bring it up for you.

My father tells the story of an old mule trader that noticed a number of fine, young sorrel mules showing up at a local auction barn. He learned they were all sired by a particular jack, whose owner had a reputation for getting quite nasty anytime someone offered to buy the animal. One day the trader asked his spotter to take him to see the beast's owner. The spotter is said to have told the trader, "I'll leave the engine running."

The mule trader made conversation with the farmer, telling him he was in the market for some four to five-year-old farm mules. The man only had yearlings, which the trader bragged on extensively. He then asked where those fine yearlings had come from. The farmer led him back to the barn and showed him the prize jack.

The trader bragged on the farmer's rock house to the point that it inspired the farmer to grant him a tour, and afterward he complimented the yearlings again. The trader never mentioned buying the jack, and the two got along so well that the farmer sent the trader off with a big sack of sassafras root.

As they left the property, the trader told his spotter, "If you ever hear of him wantin' to sell that jack, you let me know!"

A year later the trader got word that the farmer was entertaining the idea of selling the jack and promptly went to see him.

He again bragged on the farmer's stock and the rock house, and was given yet another tour. At what would have otherwise been the end of his visit he said to the farmer, "I might be mistaken, but did I hear that you were lookin' to sell that jack of yours?"

The mule trader got the jack. In fact, he didn't even buy him, he traded two Belgian mares for him.

The mule trader was shrewd enough to realize that minimizing his true objective would be the key to getting the prize jack. Had he gone onto the man's property waving a fist full of money he could not have gotten the animal any sooner. In truth, that approach would have probably precluded him from ever getting it from the stubborn farmer.

COME FROM A POSITION OF KNOWLEDGE

The second part of my colleague's statement, "I just want to know why you did it," is the most powerful. It opens the door for a suspect to explain away his behavior, which as we have just seen, many are eager to do. More importantly, saying, "I just want to know why you did it," boldly implies that the speaker already knows what has happened and who is responsible. He jumps right over the question of guilt as if that is a forgone conclusion—and of little interest, anyway. Giving the impression that you're already informed (and confident of the information) is an effective way to subdue a person's temptation to be deceptive.

A former FBI agent I know tells the story of a minor dispute that occurred in his condominium complex one evening. I was fascinated when I heard his technique for handling the matter. After visiting his residence, his daughter returned to the parking lot where she discovered a dent on the fender of her car. After examining the paint transfer left by the striking vehicle and gathering a few facts, the former agent deduced that the offender was actually a fellow tenant. He told me how he had approached the man: "You hit my daughter's car, and I want to know what you're going to do about it." Confronted with a person who seemed informed and confident of the information, the man confessed that he had bumped the car.

When it comes to getting information—and especially the truth—from others, the single most powerful thing you can do is come from a position of knowledge. Confidence is key. Speak as if you're already at third base. Start at first base, and you may never move past it.

My story about knocking on doors for wanted people relates my first experience with approaching people from a position of knowledge. Through the years since then I've used it in varying forms. The reason it works is simple: even people who will lie readily prefer not to be caught doing it.

People don't lie so they can be discovered, they lie because they want us to believe a particular point. In choosing whether to use deception, one of the deciding factors for people is the likelihood of being caught. The higher it appears to be, the less attractive deception becomes. When we give the impression we're already informed on an issue, the person we're conversing with will consider there to be a greater likelihood of their deception being recognized. As a result, they will have an increased reluctance to try deception.

But there's an important point to remember. If you're bluffing, make sure you don't say anything that will be recognized as wrong. Remember the story about Kenny, the jailed young man who thought he'd left his fingerprints all over the inside of the pizza restaurant. I was able to get his confession by showing him that I had "his print" from the scene. This worked only because Kenny believed his prints were in the business and I had been gifted with this knowledge. What if I had merely heard he was the burglar and had decided to try bluffing him into a confession by showing him a lifted fingerprint "from the scene." The outcome would have been very different if he had indeed committed the burglary, but had worn gloves when he did it. The reason my bluff with the fingerprint worked was that when I came from a position of knowledge, I was right.

The Lost Art Of Agreement

In the summer of 1994, I was working undercover in southern Missouri, running the neighborhoods of a city with an informant who tended to both think too much and talk too much, but not necessarily in that order. Like many others before him, Tommy came to help us fight the drug war because he was already a participant, but on the other side; he sold a pound of marijuana to one of my partners, then found himself in need of a little help.

Informants, specifically the ones who are working off their own crimes, are some of the most dangerous people anyone can associate with. Just ask their cousins, their best friends, their fathers, or any of the other people to whom they've introduced an undercover police officer. Their sacrifice of people close to them, people who trust them, in exchange for their own safe passage, demonstrates where they put their own well being in relation to those around them.

Knowing this, it was no surprise to me when Tommy pointed the way one day to the apartment of his ex-girlfriend. She thought so much of him at one time that unbeknownst to her husband, they had named their son after Tommy. "She can hook us up," he said eagerly.

She and her husband lived with their infant son in the attic of an old house on the east side of town. When we entered the driveway on our first visit, she was sunbathing in a chaise lounge in the front yard. She came running, obviously glad to see Tommy. He introduced her to me, then the two of them bantered back and forth as I leaned on the fence, playing the part of an uninterested wallflower. Tommy tended to be a little pushy at times, so I had given him clear orders before we left my car: "Don't bring up the subject of dope."

Though I didn't consider this approach too deeply during those days, I realize now that I was minimizing my true objective. Depending upon circumstances, I often told an informant not to initiate talk about drugs. On the first visit I thought it was enough just to be introduced to the target, build some rapport, let them get to know me, and then leave. Dropping by for no apparent reason stood to give me more credibility than barging in asking to buy drugs. Besides, I was in no hurry. If they didn't bring up the subject (which they often did), we could always come back, which we always did. The second time, at least, I wouldn't be a new face.

But if the target brought up the subject of dope, well, that was another story altogether. That was the best scenario imaginable. The target would be comfortable with the subject because he had introduced it, and we could get right to the business I had actually come for without appearing eager and therefore suspicious. To my pleasant surprise, that's just what this girl did. Within an hour and a half of meeting her, I was leaving with a half pound of marijuana wrapped in a towel under my arm.

We visited her place several more times over the following month, and I bought more marijuana. During one of the deals she proposed something new, something that I had never heard of anyone in the area dealing. Her marijuana source had a quart of liquid morphine, and she was trying to find a buyer. I told her I might be interested. "Get a price," I said, "and I'll check around with some people I know."

About two weeks passed with no word from Tommy. Informants come and go, but they do neither when you would most like them to. Tommy had left me, but thoughts of the morphine had not. I still wanted to make the deal, primarily because I've always leaned toward novelty; no one I knew had ever scored morphine. I decided to go ahead without him. After failing several times to catch her at home, one day I tried calling, and she picked up the phone.

She was friendly and talkative, but she seemed evasive when I mentioned "the stuff we talked about." Initially I suspected that discussing the matter on the phone had made her apprehensive. After my second pass at the subject, though, she finally said, "Look, I'll just level with you. I don't know you that well and I've heard some rumors about Tommy...like he's working with the cops. It would be just like that little #$%@! to do something like that. I don't mean anything personal toward you, but I've just been hearing some rumors."

What do you say to this? The natural impulse would be to try to discount the rumors and tell her that Tommy's a solid guy, or maybe show some anger at her suggestion that I was a cop, or both. But neither option seemed right.

I realized intuitively that a lot of the people who knew him well probably didn't trust Tommy completely. I certainly didn't, but then I knew something about him that his running buddies were yet to find out. Still, their faith in him was so shallow that the flimsiest rumor was enough to tip the balance against him—and me. I would have a hard time convincing this girl she should disregard what she had heard, much less disregard her instincts.

So I didn't try to. "I wasn't going to say anything, but I've heard some of the same things myself," I told her. "I'm glad you said something because I didn't really know what to believe...but if you've heard this stuff too, I'm going to stay the hell away from him." There was a pause, and then she asked, "Do you think it's true?" "I don't know," I answered. "But if it would make you feel better, I won't bring him around anymore." "That really would be better," she said.

Could anyone change positions more radically within the span of half a minute? I could hardly believe my ears! He was the one who had been bringing *me* around! One moment she essentially suggested that I could be Johnny Law, and the next *instant* she had transferred all her suspicions away from me onto Tommy. And she only knew me because *Tommy* had introduced us. Unbelievable!

I have since realized it was my agreement that disarmed her. Instead of trying to refute her statement, I jumped in and added to its momentum. Not only did it give me credibility when I suggested that I had heard the same rumors, it kept us in a state of agreement. Had I hit her with an opposing point of view, there would have been conflict. Worse, it would have been *me* who represented conflict. Would that have done anything to increase her trust in me? Absolutely not. My agreement with her case, however, eased her anxiety and put us on the same side of the issue.

The old Korean martial art of Hapkido is based upon the same principle. Instead of meeting force with force, one simply makes use of his attacker's momentum. When pushed, he pulls. When pulled, he pushes. Instead of opposing the forces exerted upon him, he redirects them and allows them to continue, making use of the energy and weight of his opponent. It takes less effort to raise a knee into an adversary coming at you than it does to throw a punch of your own.

I've found that the same principles hold true in conversation. Great success awaits us when we make use of the other person's momentum and create an air of purposeful agreement rather than instinctive conflict. It's so much easier to gain acceptance of our words when both parties to a conversation are moving in the same direction.

Most people, of course, never try this. When a person expresses thoughts or beliefs that contradict theirs, they feel inclined to engage the issues head-on. Once the "Me vs. You" rules are invoked, the chances of convincing or even swaying the other person become virtually non-existent.

Assumptive Questions—Why Start At First Base When You Can Start At Third?

If you've ever watched the direct examination of a witness, either in actual court or on the screen, you've likely seen a defense attorney come to his feet at some point and belt out, "I object, your honor, the prosecution is leading the witness!" Leading questions on direct examination are challenged because they feed answers and invite the witness to give a particular response.

Assumptive questions operate under the same premise as leading questions in that they draw the person answering toward giving a valuable answer. Assumptive questions move into action the philosophy of coming from a position of knowledge:

1) Billy, do you know who threw the rock through the window?

2) Billy, did you throw the rock through the window?

3) Billy, why did you throw the rock through the window?

Supposing that Billy threw the rock through the window, which one of these questions do you think would have the best chance of getting him to acknowledge it?

Notice that each question becomes more accusatory than the last. The first one obviously allows Billy the most latitude. He can comfortably say "no" to this one. The question doesn't imply that the identity of the rock thrower is known and it certainly bears no implication that Billy did it.

Though the second one implies that the questioner suspects Billy broke the window, it doesn't demonstrate much confidence in that suspicion. Billy can comfortably say "no." Neither of the first two questions have enough assumption of Billy's guilt to reasonably bring him to answer the questions truthfully. To be effective, a question must pressure its target. If someone is inclined to avoid the truth, we should make them work at it, not toss them softballs.

Only the third question assumes Billy's guilt. Unlike the first two, it does not invite a one-word answer. It will require Billy to put forth some effort if he wants to be deceptive.

A person questioning Billy could start off with number one, then go to two, and finally to three. But what would be the point? After asking the first two questions, it would be entirely evident to Billy that the questioner has no proof of his guilt. The escalating questions would only give the impression that the questioner is "fishing."

Even if the questioner had ironclad proof of Billy's guilt, he wouldn't want to ask question number one or two. When a person takes a position publicly, he'll resist changing it. Setting Billy up to answer "no" to either of the first two questions would make it doubly hard to get a confession from him; he would be put in the position of admitting that he is both a vandal for throwing the rock and a liar for initially denying it.

Regardless of the questioner's surety of Billy's guilt, it would be most sensible to start with question number three. It assumes his guilt, which makes the job of denial more difficult than issuing a simple "no." When we force people to work at being deceptive, we find that many of them will not choose to make the effort (and take the risk).

Which column of questions do you think would elicit the most valuable answers:

Did you see the car? or   What did the car look like?

Do you plan to take a vacation? or   Where are you going for your vacation?

Did you go to Vinnie's last night? or   Who did you see at Vinnie's last night?

Can you be there Tuesday? or   What time will you be there Tuesday?

Were you late? or   How late were you?

The questions on the left allow a person to divert the questioner with an abrupt and uninformative "no." The questions on the right demand that a valuable answer be provided.

Make it habit to phrase all your questions so that they assume the recipient has an answer. This technique will eliminate several unnecessary steps in the question-answer process and lead to more valuable and succinct answers in a shorter amount of time. Even when deception isn't a concern, assumptive questions evoke answers that are clearer, more direct, and more revealing.

Question Format: Closed vs. Open

Of the factors that determine the effectiveness of questions, including tone, content, and delivery, there is perhaps nothing more critical to their success than format. Fortunately, question format is also quite simple. Questions are either closed or open.

CLOSED QUESTIONS

Closed questions lead (or allow) the answerer to give a yes or no response: "Does Walter Jones own a .357 magnum?"

Closed questions are typically simple and straightforward and they do little to encourage detailed answers. In fact, they stifle detail. Attorneys frequently use closed questions in the courtroom, particularly during cross examinations where they want to limit or illuminate a witness's answer. A prosecutor may not want the jury or the court to hear explanations or lengthy details, so he continues to pose closed questions such as, "Did you see Walter Jones with a .357 magnum on the night of October 16?" When he asks the witness if the accused had a gun on the night of the murder, he wants the answer to be succinct and dramatic: "Yes."

There's an adage that "a good attorney never asks a question to which he doesn't know the answer." To the contrary, the rest of us routinely ask questions to which we don't know the answers. If we're seeking informative answers, why would we want to ask closed questions which plainly invite the recipient to limit the information in his response?

In the last section I gave some examples of questions that would elicit answers of little value. Take another look at the questions that were in the left column—they are closed questions:

Did you see the car?

Do you plan to take a vacation?

Did you go to Vinnie's last night?

Can you be there Tuesday?

Were you late?

There are people who can't help but give detailed answers whether we want them or not, regardless of question format. Others, though, are less forthcoming. When dealing with someone who has either chosen to be deceptive or is merely reluctant to talk, a closed question is an open invitation for an abbreviated response.

Closed questions aren't innately bad, they just need to be understood and used appropriately. There may be times when, like the attorney, we actually want to limit the answer of another person. But that should happen through intent, not accident.

OPEN QUESTIONS

Unlike closed questions, open questions entice the person answering to elaborate. In the example in the previous section, the questions in the right column were open questions:

> What did the car look like?
>
> Where are you going for your vacation?
>
> Who did you see at Vinnie's last night?
>
> What time will you be there Tuesday?
>
> How late were you?

These are better questions because they lure a person to give an answer that goes beyond a mediocre yes or no. When either truth or detail is the objective, open questions are the obvious choice.

Don't Give Them Permission

Many of the mistakes we make in conversation occur because our actions are rooted in repetition and habit rather than in logic. For instance, the way people around us phrase their speech often becomes the way we phrase our own statements. Unfortunately, we seldom stop to consider whether the way we've seen it done is actually the best way to do it. A lot of the techniques detailed in this book require you to avoid speaking impulsively, habitually, or emotionally, in favor of speaking logically and strategically. This is especially necessary with what is explained next. Whether out of habit, courtesy, or ignorance, people routinely commit an error that undermines the question-offering process; they give people permission not to answer their questions.

Because presentation is always paramount, the way we preface a question is extremely important. The words that set up a question play an ancillary role in that they also set up the expectation of how it will be answered. When we preface our questions to others with lines like these, we set low expectations for their answers:

- Can you recall...
- Can you tell me...
- Do you remember...
- Did he say anything about...
- Are you aware of...

Set-ups like these imply that the answerer may not be able to produce. Actually, they go a step beyond that. They imply that not producing an answer would be *acceptable*. When we ask a person, "Can you remember what you did on the night of June 25?" we're really pointing out to the person that he can either remember or not remember. If we're dealing with someone who'd rather not, we've given him permission. By posing the question this way, we include "not remembering" as an equal probability. Starting with words like "Can you...," conveys doubt about how much there is to learn. It allows that maybe the recipient "Can *not*...."

Even in the case of an individual who has no intention of being deceptive, questions that are introduced with these kinds of phrases don't demand much of him. Because they're weak in the expectation department, the person to whom these kinds of questions are posed won't feel any great obligation to search for the information. Even honest people sometimes like to get by with the slightest effort possible, and questions like these allow them to do just that. They can furnish a satisfactory answer without working too hard to find it. Worst of all, questions of this style are closed. They can always be fulfilled with a dull and uninformative "no."

Of all the mistakes that can be made in phrasing questions, giving another person permission to deny us an answer is at the same time the simplest and the most insidious. Though I have been aware of this potential pitfall in asking questions for years, it's something I still catch myself doing. To avoid prefacing our questions with escape hatches is a worthy effort, but it's difficult to do consistently. Try it and you'll find how deep the habit runs.

If knowing about this problem doesn't keep me from doing it on occasion, you might imagine that those who have never considered it do it all the time. Attorneys, whose livelihoods depend upon their ability to ask effective questions, violate this concept reliably. I have yet to attend a deposition in which the examining attorney didn't regularly use questions that began with "Can you recall...," and "Do you remember...," which are the two most overused and worthless prefaces. As you might guess, I've also heard a lot of respondents answer "no" to these weakly worded set-ups. The way a question is asked always establishes the expectation (great or small) of how it will be answered. Don't demand much and you won't get much.

One reason we start questions in this manner is that we're thinking, "Can he tell me?" as we ask a question of another person. That's all right to think, but that wonderment shouldn't be put into words. Our questions should assume that the person can answer our questions, and so we should preface them in a way that displays our confidence in that assumption.

So what's the alternative? That's the easy part:

- "Do you know..."
- "Can you recall..."
- "Can you tell me..."
- "Do you remember..."
- "Did he say anything about..."
- "Are you aware of..."

can all be replaced with a single set-up that's magically universal: "*Tell me....*"

These words are powerful together. They incorporate coming from a position of knowledge with the concept of assumptive questions. To say, "Tell me..." is to imply that you know the person has the answer. It also jumps straight to third base because it skips the preliminaries that enable a deceptive person to thwart you. In contrast to the aforementioned weak set-ups which give the answer-er the power to easily avoid giving a substantive answer, this phrase commands the recipient to do just what you'd like him to: *tell you.*

Which of these questions would stand the greatest chance of eliciting full and honest answers:

"Do you know about Tony's background?" or
"Tell me about Tony's background."

It's worthwhile to style questions this way even when deception isn't a concern. Phrases like these are alternatives that are just as effective—use them for variety or when "tell me" seems too forceful:

- "Who is/was/did..."
- "What is/was/did..."
- "When is/was/did..."
- "Where is/was/did..."
- "Why is/was/did..."

If these seem familiar, it's because you've probably heard or used them many times. They're the Five W's: who, what, when, where, and why. This little jingle has been used for years to remind us of the key points to cover when we gather information.

Note that there are only five. The old axiom didn't include "whether." If we want to ask a person about their knowledge of a particular subject, we shouldn't express doubts about whether they hold the information. If you seem as if you don't know *whether* the person can answer your questions, they'll be able to decide *whether* to give you the information you're requesting. Presume that they know and you'll stand a greater chance of learning what they know.

Of course, none of this guarantees that you'll get honest and complete answers every time you ask a question. But it does assure you the best chance at getting them. If someone wants to deny you information, put them in a position where they have to lie to you to do it. If you make them work at it, one of two things will happen: they won't be willing to put forth the effort or the risk to lie, or you'll have them committed to a specific account that may be verified or discounted.

If you can't get the truth, a good lie will do.
—John H. Manning

Avoid prefacing questions with phrases that give permission for useless answers. Go directly to the point and construct questions so that they demand thoughtful answers.

Don't Do The Work For Them

Ironically, when we want information from another person, it's common for us to actually offer them an answer as we ask the question. Lawyers object to these kinds of questions in the courtroom for fear that they'll lead a witness to a particular answer. Unfortunately, the rest of us often pose leading questions in ordinary conversations without even realizing it. Some examples and their alternatives:

not "Who was standing there—Basil?"
but "Who was standing there?"

not "What color was it—orange?"
but "What color was it?"

not "When did it explode—after midnight?"
but "When did it explode?"

not "Why did you do it—to retaliate for the fight on
    Thursday?"
but "Why did you do it?"

not "Where is he now—on Third Street?
but "Where is he now?"

There are several reasons to be conscious of leading questions. Though attorneys use them to get the answers they want, people who use them in conversations outside the courtroom often get responses they don't want. Instead of original answers, these questions simply ask for a confirmation of the questioner's information.

Even more devastating is the ability of the leading question to inform the other person of what we believe, know, or don't know. Suppose you asked Helen, "Where did you go last night, to Thelma's house?" The phraseology of the question would imply that you believe Helen went to Thelma's house. If she actually went to Bill's house but would prefer to have you believe she went to Thelma's, she can merely say, "Yes." She can be deceptive with slight effort and no creativity. Not only did you give her a leading question that gave away your thoughts, it was a closed question that she could easily field.

Similarly, a leading question can tell the other person what you *don't* know. When you ask Helen if she went to Thelma's last night, you will be telegraphing that you don't know where she went. When she realizes what you don't know, she'll feel more comfortable in confirming your misbelief.

Overcoming the tendency to supply answers with questions is a challenge for lawyers, police investigators, human resources managers, reporters, and countless others who ask questions for a living. For the best answers, ask naked questions that force the recipient to generate his own answers from scratch. Doing the work for them always reduces the odds of getting original, unadulterated information.

Don't Feed 'Em

We're also guilty of doing the work for them when we feed information back to a person as we ask a question. I see attorneys do this also with great frequency. When asking a question that begs for clarification or more detail concerning a previous answer, we have the opportunity to compare a new answer against an old one. A second-pass question like, "You said you were going to Mike's house when you ran into David?" is more helpful to the answerer than saying, "Tell me about the trip to Mike's house."

Don't remind a person of what they've already said, just ask your question in its simplest form. People often forget some of the details of their misrepresentations. Because false assertions come from construction rather than from recollection, a person may not repeat them the same way a second time around. Their tales were imagined, not lived. Retouching on previously answered subjects is an opportunity to evaluate two responses that concern one issue. Giving information in the question voids that opportunity.

If You Don't Want It, Don't Ask For It

Anticipation can be overwhelming. I remember my father asking me as a young boy the rhetorical question, "Where's your patience?" Kids lack patience, but adults often do too, particularly in personal conversations where we sometimes become negative and actually ask for confirmation of what we dread:

- "So, are you saying that you won't go?"
- "You don't like it, do you?"
- "Do you disagree with me?"
- "You don't love me anymore, do you?"

There are several problems with asking doomsday questions such as these. Not only are we actually *asking* the other person to commit to an outcome or position that we don't want, but remember that when a person takes a position publicly, he'll resist changing it. Also, once they've stated their thoughts, people feel freer to act upon them. Once out of the mouth, words can never be put back. When we ask a person to verify an unwanted position, we should be prepared to deal with it on a new level. The course of the conversation or the relationship may be altered from that point forward. When we fear that something bad is lurking around the corner, we want to confront it. The problem is that by doing so, we may not diffuse the problem as we'd like, we may instead solidify it.

When you suspect that the person you're conversing with holds a position you don't want, don't ask them to declare it. Continue to move forward. Instead of focusing on the ideas, decisions, or beliefs that you don't want, focus on the issue and the side of it you want them to accept. These are occasions to preserve our strategy, not offer questions that undermine our own objectives.

Don't Ask In The Negative

When discussing the bad things people impulsively do in conversation, I can't leave out what I call "asking in the negative." Whether it's due to thoughtless pessimism or just thoughtless habit, quite often we ask questions that beg for a negative result. Some examples and their alternatives:

not "You don't have any lemon juice, do you?"
but "Where's the lemon juice?"

not "He doesn't have time to see me, does he?"
but "When can I see him?"

not "You wouldn't take fifty dollars for it, would you?"
but "I'll give you fifty dollars for it."

The way a question is asked establishes the expectation (great or small) of how it will be answered. When we ask questions that *expect* negative answers, we dramatically increase the odds of getting them.

Present The Positive

"I've got good news and I've got bad news." We've all heard this line, and most of us have said it as well. It does seem that people are fascinated with bad news. Sometimes we unconsciously fall into the habit of framing what we say so that it has a negative connotation, even when there may really be nothing negative about the message.

It's easy to imagine that the way we present news has a lot to do with the way it's perceived. Instead of presenting information with a negative slant, it's just as easy to present it with a positive one:

not "We won't be able to give you five percent until August."
but "We'll be able to give you five percent in August."

not "Son, you have to eat what we're eating tonight."
but "Son, you can have some of what we're eating."

not "I don't want you to come Thursday."
but "I'd love for you to come Friday."

Each pair of statements carries the same message. One presents the point as negative and commanding, while the other presents it in a way that sounds beneficial to the listener. The way thoughts are phrased sets them up to inspire either resistance or acceptance.

Remarks that inspire resistance often do so because they focus on what *won't* happen rather than what *will*. They contain words like "can't," "aren't," "don't," or "shouldn't," which have negative undertones because each focuses on what is *excluded* from happening. Presenting the positive is simple. Say what *will* happen. Phrasing orders, requests, or statements this way will give them the ring of opportunity rather than the thud of restriction.

Don't Ask A Multiple Question

Asking a multiple question can be disastrous. Members of the Washington press corps, whose mission (theoretically) relies on adept questioning, do this consistently. Examples can be seen in any presidential news conference. Few reporters in the room are pointed to by the president, and when one finally is chosen, he tries to make the most of the opportunity. Frequently, the questions are styled something like this: "Mr. President, have you had an opportunity to speak with the ambassador regarding the demonstrations, and do you think that the events will have an effect on U.S. relations with the Russians? And is it true that as a result of the recent developments in that country you have considered canceling your visit scheduled for later this year?"

Reporters who ask long-winded questions get little in return and for several reasons. For example, this one actually contains three questions. Because it lacks focus, an honest answerer may not remember all its parts, and a deceptive answerer may choose the parts he is most comfortable with. Further, an ambiguous answer won't stand out as such, because the question itself was ambiguous. Deception aside, asking a multiple question allows the answerer too much latitude.

The nature of some conversations can lure us into issuing multiple questions. Heated conversations in which emotion dominates reason are notorious for this. In our fervor to score against the other side, we fire away with a barrage of questions. Instead of pinning a person down, though, we actually give them the space they need. Big questions, ones that have multiple warheads, aren't devastating. They don't confine, they liberate.

Good questions put demands upon the receiver. They obligate him, place an expectation upon him, even hem him in. Effective questions are narrow in scope and concise. The latitude of a question becomes the latitude for its answer.

But Nothing...

Mothers are notorious for giving orders topped off with, "And I don't want to hear any *buts*..." The reason for the admonition is simple. Even people who have never been students of interpersonal communication realize that "but" is a negative word. It signals non-acceptance and is usually an introduction to a contradictory statement. When used as a transition in a phrase, "but" negates whatever precedes it:

- "I understand what you're saying, but..."
- "That's a good point, but..."
- "You could be right, but..."

Each statement expresses approval that is immediately called into question by "but...." What follows that word isn't specifically important. Whatever follows, we know that it won't be supporting the first part of the sentence.

People commonly speak this way. Perhaps it's a way of being courteous, by acknowledging the other person's point before delivering our own, or it may simply be another unquestioned habit.

During the early 1990's, I noticed a trend in law enforcement to school officers in verbal techniques designed to diffuse, rather than escalate, potentially confrontational situations. I stated in the first chapter that until recent years, no one had paid much attention to developing the conversational skills of police officers. The advent and popularity of these programs was a visible example that a change in attitude was occurring. Law enforcement agencies were acknowledging that learning to communicate effectively with the public was just as important to the street officer's success as learning to shoot, write a report, or win a fight.

While the courses represented a step in the right direction, some of them depended largely on redirecting behavior through the use of "but." They focused on appeasing the adversary by expressing agreement or understanding, then moving into whatever the officer's objectives are: "That's understandable, *but*...I've got a job to do, so you'll need to come with me."

The problem with this approach is that by design it makes it apparent that the officer and the person to whom he is speaking have objectives that are at odds with one another. The insertion of "but" pits the parties against each other: "You've got your angle, *but*...I've got mine," is the impression given. These statements are supposed to appreciate the viewpoint of an officer's adversary, and thus calm him down. Any empathy, though, is totally washed away by the second half of the statement which is introduced by the word "but."

What if instead of putting your ideas at odds with the other person's, you could attach yours to theirs? What if you could link and associate the things you *want* someone to accept to that which they *already* accept? Again, agreement gets us moving in a common direction and that empowers us to have much greater influence than if we're playing tug of war. The negative connotation of "but..." can be avoided by using "and..." instead:

"I understand what you're saying, but..." or
"I understand what you're saying, and..."

The second statement allows the speaker to hitch his proposition to something the other person believes. The use of "and..." gives the feel of agreement even when there may be none yet. By linking what they already accept to what we want them to accept, the job of convincing others is made easier.

Save Your Thoughts and Opinions

People like to be accepted by other people. They like to fit in, especially where groups are concerned, and they like to avoid embarrassment. When an opinion or belief is stated in front of others, a benchmark is established. While some will boldly go against it, there are a greater number who won't. They may express a similar viewpoint as the one already stated because they don't want to go against the grain, appear wrong, or be impolite.

The relationship between two people has a great deal to do with the stands they take. A supervisor who expresses an opinion and then asks a newly employed subordinate about his thoughts on the subject shouldn't expect an original and honest answer. This isn't to say that the employee would be choosing to be deceptive in the classical sense, but if he doesn't hold the boss's viewpoint, he's put in the position of contradicting his superior's opinion. Most people would avoid the discomfort of doing that.

There is a vast difference between influencing another person's opinions or beliefs and influencing what they *say* about their opinions or beliefs. Peer pressure, even among adults, can move people to agree with viewpoints they don't necessarily hold, or sit quiet as something they do believe in is disparaged. Statements like these don't elicit the best answers:

- "I think Stewart would be the only logical choice for the Senate seat. What do you think?"

- "I'm pretty sure that happened on a Tuesday. When do you think it was?"

- "That was the worst movie I've ever seen. What did you think of it?"

This error is caused by saying more than is necessary, a pitfall that finds its way into many areas of conversation. Each of these statements would be more effective at getting a genuine answer from the other person if we simply used the second half of each:

- "What do you think about Stewart for Senate?"

- "When do you think it was?"

- "What did you think of the movie?"

Withholding our opinions, beliefs, or recollections is vital to getting honest answers. When we express our thoughts first, we run the risk of tainting the remarks of another person, even of those who had no intention of being deceptive.

...

When we covered the subject of influencing others, it was with the aim of influencing them in ways that contribute to our objectives. Clearly, the way we state ourselves has the potential to undermine our objectives, even as we're trying to advance them. To get honest and complete answers from others, we have to make certain our questions are absent prejudice toward a particular answer and that they encourage, not stifle, the return of useful information.

The Mechanics Of Great Questioning

Many police officers fail at interrogation because they are unable to drop their face of authority. Just as we can't influence the behavior of others by ordering them to accept our wishes, ideas, or beliefs, neither can we get another person to be truthful simply by commanding them. Officers of the law are accustomed to being in control, taking charge, and never taking "no" for an answer. Interrogations, then, present quite a challenge. They are mental jousting matches. A suspect can say whatever he chooses, ignore an officer's words, or even end the conversation. For a lot of officers, the frustration of dealing with a suspect under these conditions is more than they care to tolerate and their patience is sapped before results begin to appear.

The information in this chapter, even more so than the others, is adapted directly from the interrogation room. Some of the information is still best suited for accusatory, rather than casual, conversation. These theories and techniques are more obtuse than concrete, more about strategy and concept than about specific words.

Conversation, like interrogation, is much less frustrating when we have a grasp on the components that underlie it. While the last chapter focused on phrasing questions so that they elicit useful answers, this chapter deals with the subtext of questioning, interpreting responses, and even the power of silence.

Deny Them The "No"

When a person openly states his opinion or position on a subject, he will be slow to recant it. This phenomenon is directly tied to ego, of course. When we've committed to a position publicly, we have a hard time turning on ourselves.

This is also true with denials but for reasons that go beyond ego. When interrogating suspects, I found that getting a confession was always doubly hard when the person had denied some issue relating to the crime. Without fail, the guilty people who made statements like, "I wasn't there," or "I don't know what you're talking about," early in an interview were the hardest to obtain confessions from. This was because they had taken a position publicly— even if only in front of one person—and to reverse that position would have made them a liar. Amazingly, even a crook doesn't want to look like a liar.

At some point, I realized that allowing a suspect to deny his guilt was dramatically reducing my odds of getting a confession. I changed my strategy. From that point on, I refused to allow a suspect to proclaim a position that was against my objectives. Getting confessions is difficult enough—why would I want to allow a suspect to paint himself into a corner, only to spend the rest of my efforts trying to talk him out of it?

My policy became one of interference. When a person I was interviewing started to take a position that I didn't want, such as denying involvement, presence, knowledge, or anything else I would have to overcome, I interrupted. I cut in and asked another question. I changed the subject. I said, "Hold it," stood up and opened the door, looked out, and then came back to my seat. Anything that broke the suspect's stride and allowed me to redirect the course of conversation my way was an attractive alternative to hearing him proclaim a position that would set up yet another obstacle for me. I enjoyed great success with this technique.

Strategic interference applies in other settings as well. For instance, the last words a salesman wants to hear a prospect say are, "I'm not interested, thanks." Even if he's ultimately able to overcome this objection, why would he want to allow it to be erected in the first place? Not only will he have to work to close the sale as usual, but he'll first have to get this person to recant his publicly stated position.

When it's apparent that a person is about to take a position that will become an obstacle, it's time for a diversion. It's much easier to get a person to take the position we want if we can keep him from declaring an opposing one.

There will be times when a person proclaims an undesirable position before there's an opportunity to avert it. Unfortunately, when someone takes a position that we disagree with or is at odds with our objectives, our first impulse is to zero in on their statement and try to overturn it directly. More often than not, this instantly puts the other person in the position of defending their point or statement, further entrenching their commitment.

Rather than attacking specific objections, a salesman selling Whiz-me-nots should continue on his course, unaffected by an unwanted declaration. He can talk about the features. He can talk about how the device will improve production. He can talk about the savings the prospective customer will surely see after using them just a short while. He might even go back to rapport building and lighten the pressure by moving on to something unrelated for a few minutes, perhaps something that he knows fascinates the prospect. Allowing oneself to be derailed into a debate over a person's objections is unlikely to result in him deciding to buy a pallet of product. In fact, it may well convince him that he doesn't want any at all.

To Maximize...Minimize

People confide in those that they like, trust, or respect. They also confide in people who aren't likely to judge them harshly or look down upon what they have done. When dealing with suspects, a favorite police interrogation technique centers on minimizing intent, motive, or moral seriousness of the crime. Though what someone has done may be horrendous, minimizing their actions (or decisions) makes owning up a lot easier. Consider these two statements and imagine which would be more likely to elicit an honest response from a person who had done something he'd rather not own up to:

1) "What you did was pathetic. How can you look at your self in the mirror?"

2) "We all make mistakes. I know how easily these things can happen."

Particularly when we're upset with someone or disgusted with what they've done, we impulsively want to admonish them and vent our anger. The problem is that when we react impulsively, we blatantly convey our disapproval of the person's behavior. Who wants to step up and admit to something that another person has just deemed objectionable?

To get another person to be open and honest, we need to lower the threshold so that their opinions, thoughts, or conduct can get through the door of acceptability. Statement #2 does this effectively from several angles at once:

first segment: "We all make mistakes."
translation: "You're just like the rest of us—we all do it."

To say "We all make bad decisions," would still imply that this person is "like the rest of us." But that would brand their activity "bad" and hold them to a greater level of intent by calling it a "decision." What would you rather admit to, a decision or a mistake?

second segment: "I know how easily these things can happen."
translation: "I won't judge you."

This line vaguely implies that the speaker himself may have made "mistakes" in the past. Putting ourselves on an equal moral plane with another person breeds comfort, rapport, and honesty.

Minimizing how bad or how important someone's poor conduct is will go a long way toward getting them to talk about it. This is an approach that goes hand in hand with rationalization, something at which humans have become expert. We minimize *what* we did, then rationalize *why* we did it. Putting our conduct through both of these processes severely dilutes whatever feelings of guilt or responsibility originally existed. Allowing others the latitude to do this, despite its objectionable feel, can produce results when we want them to talk openly about what they've done.

"I'll Gladly Pay You Tuesday For A Flesh Wound Today"

When I questioned suspects, I always found it best to start at a distance and work my way in. It's easier to get someone to admit they were simply in town the night of the murder than it is to get them to admit they were right where it happened. Once they've admitted being in town, it's a little easier to get them to acknowledge they were on the east side of town. Once they've committed to being on the east side of town, we might come from a position of knowledge and ask, "Is there any reason someone would tell us they saw your car on Elm Street that night?" A guilty person would likely allow just enough to keep from being caught in a lie: "I don't know. I can't tell you everywhere I drove that night."

Crooks are notorious for volunteering to take a flesh wound in hopes of avoiding the body hit. They bargain, conceding just enough information to get them through the moment, hoping that the interrogator will be satisfied they are truthful:

- "I drove the car, but I didn't know what they were doing inside the house."
- "I broke in, but I didn't set the fire."
- "I was there earlier. He was fine when I left him."
- "I bought some stuff, but I didn't steal anything from the store."
- "I might have pushed her, but I never hit her."
- "I might have done some things in the past, but I didn't do this."

When a complete and truthful answer would be detrimental, people have a tendency to admit just enough to satisfy the situation and little more. Admitting mistakes, failures, or crimes is difficult. When a person admits to something that's against his self-interest, he may only be throwing a bone in hopes that you will take it and leave.

Since people have an easier time coming clean with peripheral issues, it's best to start with those. A sharp Whiz-me-not sales rep wouldn't walk into a business and have his first words be, "Would you like to buy a pallet of Whiz-me-nots?" He would greet the manager, converse with him, establish rapport, and determine his interests and desires. In sales, at the office, or at home, patience pays. Wading in slowly can be time well spent.

Three Strikes, You're Out!

A person's avoidance of giving a direct answer to a question can be a reliable sign of deception, though in all fairness, it's not uncommon for an honest person to fail in giving a direct answer. If we were to record and then transcribe a typical social conversation, upon reading it we would see it doesn't flow like a well written novel. Especially in casual settings, our conversations are often disjointed. Thoughts occur to us and we veer off after them in unforeseen directions, other participants interrupt with their own contributions, and the original point upon which we began speaking is lost in the process. It's the inevitable nature of conversation.

Because of this phenomenon, we need a reliable technique for determining whether a person failing to answer our casual question is refusing to answer or is merely losing focus. One technique for making a determination is what I term "three strikes, you're out." If we receive a non-answer after asking a question on the same point three times, we can reliably presume that the individual is avoiding an answer and thus being deceptive. It's best to phrase the questions differently each time and to separate them by several minutes, at the least. The less obvious the efforts, the more effective they'll be.

The reliability of this technique is dependant upon environment. It is most effective when two people are conversing alone and without distractions. If those conditions don't exist, the exercise should be delayed or the results should not be considered conclusive.

This technique is founded on the fact that with the exception of pathological liars, *everyone* wants to avoid lying. If asked, "Did you go to Diane's last night," the deceptive person will likely start off with the least amount of deceit possible. Rather than responding with an outright lie by saying "No," he might instead say, "Did I go to Diane's last night?" Such an answer would hold two advantages: 1) it buys time, and 2) for the moment, the respondent will have avoided committing himself to an answer that might be proven false later.

In a police interrogation, an investigator could press harder for an answer. But in social or business contexts, that won't be appropriate. The conversation must move on. Casually, though, an issue can be revisited: "Have you been by Diane's house lately?" While it might be truthful, an answer such as, "Well, I've been pretty busy lately," would constitute strike number two. Three distinct non-answers would be a sign that the person doesn't care to answer the question.

Avoidance is the most prevalent form of deception. It can offer the same results as an outright lie, while requiring less effort, commitment, and risk. Since people prefer to use the least amount of deception possible, avoidance is where most of the deceptive ones begin.

Stacked Questions

When a police detective sits down with a suspect, his surety of that person's guilt can vary widely. Some cases have a clearly defined and undeniable suspect. If the suspect, for instance, is caught committing a crime on a surveillance tape, there won't be much question as to whether the investigator has the right man.

Other cases—in fact, a great many of them—will be muddy, to say the least. A person may be a suspect because an informant claims to have heard him bragging about a robbery, or perhaps his car was seen leaving the area immediately before a fire was discovered. In these instances, the interview and interrogation process will serve first to identify the right suspect and second to get that person's confession. When an interrogator is less than certain he is talking to *the* suspect, his ability to ask effective questions will be critical in helping him to satisfy himself that he has the right person.

A good investigator knows how to stack his questions. This refers not to the way the questions are arranged but to how each is constructed. By posing questions formed the right way, an interrogator can interpret a great deal more from the answers that come back to him.

The following are examples of the kinds of questions commonly used by interrogators to help gauge the guilt of a suspect. Each is followed by responses that typify innocence and guilt:

> Who could have done this?
>> Innocent: "I'm not sure/I don't know."
>> Guilty: "It could have been anybody." (Avoids narrowing the suspect pool)

> How do you think this happened?"
>> Innocent: "I don't know."
>> Guilty: Offers ideas on how it might have occurred.

Would you make a good suspect?

> Innocent: May allow that someone could consider
> him a suspect (particularly in cases such
> as internal theft).
>
> Guilty: "No." (Anybody but me!)

Have you ever thought of doing something like this?

> Innocent: "No."
>
> Guilty: "I may have *thought* about it."

Do you think the person who did this is a good person that just made a mistake?

> Innocent: "I have no idea/I doubt it/no."
>
> Guilty: "Probably."

Would you be willing to pay the money back if that would put this whole thing to rest?

> Innocent: "No way! I didn't steal anything!"
>
> Guilty: Allows for the possibility of making
> restitution.

Can you understand why someone would do this?

> Innocent: "No."
>
> Guilty: Allows for reasons for the behavior.

How do you think the person who did this should be punished?

> Innocent: "They should go to jail."
>
> Guilty: "They should probably get some help/have to
> pay the money back/pay a fine," or "I don't
> know."

How would you do on a polygraph test?"
>   Innocent: "Fine," or "I'd pass it."
>   Guilty: "I don't know," (or my personal favorite and
>   a common answer from the guilty: "I
>   don't know, I've never taken one before.")

Are you sure? (as a follow-up to any question)
>   Innocent: "Yes."
>   Guilty: Hesitates before answering, and/or "What
>   do you mean?" or "Am I sure?"

The innocent have no reservations about condemning behavior or suggesting harsh punishments. The guilty, on the other hand, tend to minimize the wrongdoing and refrain from judging it too harshly. They also want to avoid falling into the suspect pool.

These examples illustrate how a person's connection to an incident affects his discussion of the subject. This is what makes the guilty answer differently from the innocent. An individual who has a personal stake in a matter will discuss that subject differently than will a person who is uninvolved.

These questions can be adapted to a variety of situations. It is a conceptual way of thinking, more than a concrete set of questions. The best questions call on a person to render judgment on the behavior, motivation, or punishment of the person responsible for whatever is being discussed. They need not be accusatory. We use questions like the ones above not to obtain explicit confessions but rather to judge guilt through the reasonableness of a person's responses.

The Convenience Of Forgetting

Our lack of memory can be an aggravation when we want to recall something for ourselves, and it can be a convenience when we'd rather not recall something for someone else.

Since no one can prove absolutely what another person can or can't remember, lack of memory is a popular method of deception. Like opinion, memory is subjective. It belongs to us individually and no one can examine it without our consent. If we do choose to expose it, we can edit, abbreviate, or distort it first. We can even tell others that a given memory has been deleted from our files if we'd rather not discuss, debate, or defend the subject. In most cases, not being able to remember is a pretty effective way to avoid dealing with past events, particularly ones that are embarrassing or detrimental.

Despite the frequency with which it is declared, there are only two legitimate reasons for a healthy person not being able to remember something:

1) The event was insignificant
2) The event occurred long ago

The significance of an event affects whether we store it in our memory and how long we will keep it there. If you were to witness a busy highway bridge exploding and falling into a river, that event would undoubtedly be recorded in your memory for a long time. But what if the bomber himself had happened to be alongside you at a stop light as he left the scene? Although you saw his car, even looked at his face, you would probably remember nothing about him. Because he was just another passing motorist, he would have been insignificant to you at the time, and as such would have simply not been worth remembering.

The recentness of an event also plays a substantial role in determining whether we remember it or not. You may have experienced incidents that were significant to you when they occurred and even for a time afterward, yet you can't recall them today. A cavity filled at a dentist's office, a childhood argument with a friend, or a car accident you passed on the way home ten years ago could be examples. Events like these earn a place in our memories for a short while, but most are eventually shelved indefinitely. In evaluating whether a person's lack of memory is genuine, consider the reasonableness of their claim. First note the event's significance and second, its recentness. The longer ago an event occurred, the more significant it will need to be in order to be remembered. Something insignificant that happened very recently, though, may still be remembered easily.

Subject matter is another consideration in deciding whether lack of memory is real or convenient. Does the person recall points that pose no threat to him, but seem to find it difficult to recall more pertinent information? Perhaps he remembers what the weather was like on the night of June 2, where he ate, when he left the hotel, what he was wearing, and what time he arrived home. Given that, would it be reasonable that he would be unable to recall who he was with that evening? When a person has vivid recollection of points that don't damage his interests, yet can't recall ones that might, be suspicious.

I often found that a suspect could recount a complete and perfect alibi, down to the last detail. It wasn't uncommon for me to be questioning someone about a crime that happened weeks before yet hear a confident recitation of where this person was, who he was with, and what they did on the date of the crime. I usually determined the veracity of the suspect's memory by listening to all the details and then asking him to tell me about the day prior to that one. Then I'd ask about the day after the one in question. It was amazing to see the lack of detail in their recollections of the days that surrounded the original one we had discussed. It was often the case that they could remember nothing of substance about the days surrounding the crime, but had everything down pat for the day it occurred.

Though people can legitimately have trouble remembering, we should always beware when we hear these kinds of responses, particularly when they are said repeatedly in a single conversation:

- "I don't remember."
- "Not that I can think of."
- "I can't recall."
- "I can't say."

Always consider the significance of the subject being discussed, its recentness, the threat it might pose to the person who's having memory trouble, and the frequency with which he uses these kinds of phrases.

Dissect And Reverse

Though people may jump around a bit in telling about a first-hand experience, they generally do it in chronological sequence. Because we live chronologically, we tend to recall events of life chronologically.

But deceptive people tend to be less chronological in their telling of what occurred. This is because they didn't live the details they are recounting. Instead of following the chronology of events, the deceptive tale follows its creator's imagination. As he speaks, the deceptive person often realizes that a detail was omitted and will jump backward chronologically to include the missed point. Such additions are usually included to make a story more believable, and may have little relevance to, or impact upon, the overall tale.

Though it may not be chronological, a deceptive story will have its own sequence. One way to test the authenticity of a story is to reverse it. After the conclusion of a person's account of an event, we typically have an opening to ask questions. We can bring up something from the story and ask what happened before it, then ask what happened prior to that. Depending upon the nature of the conversation, we might be able to talk about the story in reverse fashion all the way back to the beginning. This can be done by starting at the end and working back to the middle, or starting at the middle and working back to the beginning. This should be done under the guise of curiosity and clarification, not of accusation.

Truthful statements are easily reversed by the teller, deceptive ones are not. When we have lived through an event, we know it forward, backward, or sideways, and should have no trouble in recounting it from any angle. But deceptive statements fall apart under the wear and tear of this exercise. A person who tries to reverse a deceptive story will lose his way, change parts of the story, or even omit pieces of it. A deceptive story won't hold together because the teller didn't live it.

We can also repeat back a part of the story for confirmation, but omit or alter a detail. If the story is truthful, the teller will correct us. If the detail was deceptive, he may not catch the omission. Our experiences are vivid because they were real. Fabrications were never real, so the creator often fails to notice when they're adulterated or removed altogether from his tale.

Interestingly, a secondhand story also has the attributes of a deceptive story. When a person repeats an account that someone else has lived, they tend to lose some of the event's natural chronology and diminish or enhance details they might not had they lived the event themselves. Like a deceptive one, a secondhand story will not hold up to dissection and reversal.

Ask Them To Put It In The Speaker's Words

There will be occasions when a person relates the details of a conversation they had with a third party. Regardless of the subject, these accounts are typically presented in a style such as this:

"He told me that the deal was off. They wanted to get out of the contract. He said they didn't like the raw product we were shipping and he thinks they can get a better deal with Acme anyway."

Note the viewpoint. It's through the eyes of the person who is speaking, not the person who originally spoke. Instead of getting the message as it was originally intended, we are only getting the listener's translation. People inadvertently filter, distort, or fail to record information that they hear others speak, and this becomes evident when they repeat that information to others.

To avoid missing out on the original message, ask the person who's giving the highlights this: "Tell me what he said to you. *What were his words?*" It's amazing to hear the difference when a person conveys the message *as it was told to them.* The same conversation might take on an entirely different feel:

"He said, 'Although we've had a few problems with some of your product, you've always been quick to replace it. Your company has given great service and we'd be staying with you if it weren't for the discounts Acme's offering just so we'll give them a try. I think we'll eventually be back.'"

What a difference! The first statement was nothing more than an interpretation. The second was told from the viewpoint of the original speaker.

This technique is invaluable with regard to people who would deceive us about what another person told them. It's easier to generate a deceptive statement through one's own viewpoint than it is to edit the actual words of another person as one repeats them.

I worked a case in which I found this technique incredibly helpful. Several associates and I were doing some background work for an upcoming civil trial. During one of the interviews our attorney asked the witness, "What was the conversation?" The witness replied, "He told me that this guy came in and bought some beer and then left." Though I didn't think the witness was being deceptive, it was obvious he wasn't making a great effort to be thorough. I wasn't satisfied that we were getting an accurate portrayal of what had happened. So I asked, "Tell me what he said to you, what were his words?" This time the witness said, "He told me, 'This doesn't concern you, this was my mistake. I'm the one who's at fault. You don't need to worry.'"

Both of the witness's renditions concerned the same conversation. The first one was told through the witness's own viewpoint and the second actually recalled the speaker's words as they were originally intended to be heard. If we can obtain it, the latter version will always be more informative.

Visit...And Revisit

In every conversation where truth is to be evaluated, a baseline should be established at the outset. Start by determining whether the other person is extroverted or introverted, which plane of navigation he is operating in, and more importantly, which direction his eyes break when going to recollection and construction.

As this is being done, notice the associations between subjects and the verbal and physical symptoms they cause. Did the mention of his grandfather cause this visual person's eyes to drop down? Did he laugh inappropriately at the mention of a serious subject?

Having an awareness of these symptoms has a two-fold benefit. Signs like the ones I've just described provide immediate feedback, a conversational barometer. The eyes dropping down indicates a shift to an emotional state. An ill-timed laugh indicates discomfort or nervousness. We can draw immediate feedback on how the other person is reacting to what we're saying, which provides not only a gauge for deception, but also some direction for how to proceed with the conversation.

By being aware of the association between topics and responses, we can develop a strategy to move the conversation in the direction of our objectives. If we realize that talking about this person's grandfather puts him in an emotional state, then we might want to revisit that subject later to bring down defenses and provide an avenue for gaining acceptance of our points. The kinesthetic plane, after all, is the one where people are more open to us and with us.

If the person laughs nervously at the mention of a recent theft from the store vault, that's worth noting. Maybe he took the money, maybe he didn't. But most people don't laugh when they hear about stolen money. Revisiting this subject again might yield more symptoms that would help in judging the person's truthfulness.

Silence Is A Weapon

Talking can get you into more trouble than it can get you out of. The thousands of men and women sitting in penitentiaries around the United States who made admissions or confessions to cops would agree. Talking seemed right at the moment; they've since had time to reconsider.

The discomfort of silence is one cause of people speaking words they later regret. The discomfort silence brings is inversely related to the level of familiarity between two parties in conversation. Silence between good friends is comfortable. Silence between two people who have just met is not.

During my years of questioning suspects, I came to realize that my number one struggle was with myself, not the person I was conversing with. I spent so much energy building rapport, asking questions to build a baseline for responses, "denying them the no," and continually adjusting strategy, that sometimes I talked too much. To hear something incriminating, I had to stop and allow the suspect some air time.

What I realized was that I was uncomfortable with silence. I was, after all, the host of the show. I had asked this person to come to my office. I had started a conversation. I felt obligated to talk, to hold up my end of the deal.

The day I understood that I was uncomfortable with silence, I also understood that I had a new weapon. I had been breaking the silence to relieve myself of the discomfort it brings and in doing that, I had been saving the other guy. I wasn't allowing the silence to get to the point where it made *him* uncomfortable enough to speak. If one of us was going to break the silence—and one always will—I vowed to make sure it was always the other guy from then on, not me.

True silence in conversation is seldom experienced because it seldom happens. When silence starts to extend, someone usually jumps in with a remark before the situation becomes dire—and it becomes dire quickly. If you doubt me, try this: the next time you meet someone, try silence. After the initial greetings, just nod or smile when appropriate. Be pleasant, but don't say anything when the silence comes. There are two things that will absolutely happen if you do this: 1) neither of you will feel comfortable, and 2) if you are determined not to break the silence, the other person will.

I've found that when a person makes a silly remark or one they later regret, it's often the result of their nervous inclination to fill silence. It's ironic that people will allow the perceived embarrassment of silence to push them into bonafide embarrassment.

The use of extended silence works best not at the beginning of a conversation, but after the niceties are out of the way and some degree of rapport is established. We never want our silence to be taken as insolence, arrogance, or a rejection of the other person. We don't want to "give 'em the big freeze," as Bernard P. Fife once did a state patrol captain. Silence has to be employed naturally, not in a way that disintegrates the situation into an obvious battle of wills. This may be easiest to do when we're somewhat reserved from the onset of conversation, so that our silence won't be seen as an abrupt change of behavior.

Silence is a weapon. In a conversation where silence has fallen upon the participants, both will feel discomfort. The result will be that one will reach his threshold of tolerance and then break the silence. The other one will probably learn something.

What Did He Say?

On June 15, 1933, William Hamm, Jr. walked from his St. Paul, Minnesota, brewing company toward his nearby mansion for a late lunch. As he crossed the street near the corner of Minnehaha and Greenbrier, a tall distinguished looking man in his late fifties greeted him and reached to shake his hand. As the pair met, a black Hudson sedan came to the curb next to them, another man appeared on Hamm's other side, and he was pushed into the car. The distinguished looking man in the coat and tie was no businessman, it was Charlie Fitzgerald, deemed by one FBI memo as "one of the shrewdest bank burglars and robbers in the country." The man in the chauffeur's cap at the wheel of the Hudson, it would be later learned, was none other than Public Enemy Number One, the notorious Alvin "Creepy" Karpis of the Barker-Karpis Gang.

No strangers to strategy themselves, the Barker-Karpis Gang had planned the kidnap of beer magnate William Hamm in great detail. They imported a Capone mob enforcer from Chicago to head the caper. For a $25,000 cut of the expected ransom, they retained the services of a member of the St. Paul Police Department's Kidnap Detail, so they would be abreast of the Department's investigative efforts. Karpis would later recount the depth of their efforts in his autobiography, *The Alvin Karpis Story:* "We made almost daily trips into St. Paul to case Hamm's brewery and home. We mastered every last detail of the layouts of both places and spent hours studying Hamm's habits. We got to know so much about the guy that I was sick of him long before the kidnapping."

The extra trouble paid off. On June 17, the gang received the $100,000 ransom without a hitch, and they released Hamm uninjured two days later.

One month later, members of Chicago's Touhy Gang, rivals of the Capone outfit, were arrested with a cache of weapons after an automobile accident in Elkhorn, Wisconsin. Based upon items found in their car and statements from witnesses who said the men resembled the Hamm kidnappers, professional thug Roger Touhy and three associates were charged with the abduction.

Despite weak evidence and the fact that Hamm himself acknowledged the suspects didn't look or sound like his kidnappers, the Justice Department moved forward with the case at the insistence of FBI Director J. Edgar Hoover. Frustrated with U.S. Attorney Lewis Drill's doubts about the case, Hoover wrote in a confidential memo, "I don't like Drill's attitude. We have the right people, I think."

We know, of course, that they did not have the right people. A further examination of Hoover's statement demonstrates that he himself likely realized this, even as the trial was moving forward.

When Hoover wrote, "We have the right people, I think," he was trying to demonstrate that he had unwavering confidence in the guilt of the Touhy Gang. At first glance the remark seems to be a straightforward endorsement of their guilt, with no signs of doubt. But was that the case?

The statement is made of two parts: "We have the right people," and "I think." Ending with "I think" was Hoover's way of coming back and reaffirming the first part, "We have the right people." In reality, adding "I think" doesn't buttress his assertion that they had the right people, it tempers it. Had he been wholly satisfied that the Touhy Gang was responsible for the Hamm kidnapping he could simply have said, without qualification, "We have the right people." People always convey what they mean regardless of whether they say it expressly.

Indicators Of Conviction

Through experience I've found that there are three levels of conviction:

"I think"
"I believe"
"I know"

"I THINK"

Suppose you and a friend are trying to find a particular address. Your friend, seated on the passenger side of the car, tells you to take a left at the next stop light and adds, "This is the right street, I think." Based upon that remark, would you be entirely confident that he was sure of the street? Probably not. His inclusion of "I think" would temper his assertion that "This is the right street." He would be discreetly allowing for the possibility of being wrong.

"I think" reflects subjectivity, and so it is typically used in statements of personal opinion. If a person says, "I think Bob's a jerk," or "I think that's a bad idea," they are citing thoughts that are their own, ones which can't necessarily be proven to others. One can say, "I think green is an ugly color," but the speaker realizes this is merely his own opinion and one that has no provability with anyone else unless they just happen to share the opinion.

The lowest endorsement a person can give to his assertions of fact is "I think." While it doesn't necessarily mean that the speaker is deceptive, realize that when used in a purported statement of fact, the phrase demonstrates a shortage of conviction.

"I BELIEVE"

Although this term is still a subjective one, it does show a higher level of conviction than "I think." When someone attaches "I believe" to a remark, it often means that they have both a slightly higher level of faith in what they have said and in some instances a more emotional connection to the thought.

"I KNOW"

To his disappointment, famed psychotherapist Carl Jung was long ignored by both Catholics and Protestants and his views on religion were a subject of some debate. During a televised BBC interview in 1961, the reporter asked Jung whether he believed in God. He paused and said, "I do not need to believe; I know."

On its face, this could be taken as Jung's confirmation that he did indeed believe in God. His saying "I know" could under-standably be construed to mean, "I know God exists." Perhaps that was the case.

It's just as possible, though, that Jung was remarking on the broader issue of "believing" versus "knowing," without actually addressing the question of his thoughts on God. Jung was known as a man who either "knew" a thing existed, "knew" it did not exist, or allowed for a hypothesis of how it could exist. To his way of think-ing, merely "believing" had no significance. He relied on experience for what he knew; if he had not experienced a thing, then for him it did not exist.

"Knowing" is the highest display of conviction we can give to our words. To say that you "know" something means that it has been proven to your satisfaction, and you are confident that it can be proven to others. This is the most objective of the three levels of conviction. It is based less on opinion and more on fact than either of the other two.

Here is perhaps the greatest indicator of how strong know-ing is: the term is generally not even spoken. When we have full and unmitigated confidence in what we say or write, we don't feel the need to either qualify or over-endorse it. We can simply say, "That's wrong," or "This is the right street," or "God exists."

When you hear others use any of these indicators of convic-tion, consider the statements to which they are attached. Suppose you're looking over a used car and you ask the owner if he would consider taking less than the advertised price. If he responds, "It's worth what I'm asking, I think," then you should conclude that it could be had for less. He has shown weakness. What he actually means is that *he* thinks it's worth the asking price, but he's not con-fident that it is in objective terms. There would be quite another meaning if he answered, "It's worth what I'm asking." That would demonstrate that he "knows" that the car is worth the asking price.

Capturing The Meaning

We as humans are blessed with quick minds, but at the same time handicapped somewhat by mouths that can't keep up with them. People are able to think about 500 words per minute, but only able to speak about 125. This results in what I call the "funnel effect." If you could see it occurring, it would resemble the Skipper and Gilligan when they tried to go through a doorway simultaneously—too much material for the outlet.

Our minds are constantly producing thoughts, some of which we choose to keep private, some of which we choose to release. When conversing with other people, much of our mental energy is dedicated to sorting our thoughts. Which do we keep; which do we transmit? We want to portray ourselves or a subject a certain way. We want to be convincing. Perhaps we want to avoid the truth. Under normal circumstances this is a manageable task. But oftentimes there are other factors to deal with as we attempt to carry out the mission. What if we're in a job interview? What if we're debating an issue in front of a group?

Situations inevitably arise that tax our abilities to do a good job filtering the information we release. When this occurs, the thoughts we choose to release may get polluted with fragments of the thoughts we intended to keep behind. Sometimes we let things slip that everyone immediately recognizes. More often, however, the fragments are so seemingly insignificant that the average person affords them no attention. It's easy to see this, for instance, in the examples just given. Most people wouldn't appreciate the significance of "I think" versus "I know."

The fact that people let more information escape their mouths than they intend (or even realize) is what makes everything in this book possible. Their doing so generates a virtual gold mine of information for us to pick through—so long as we know what to look for and how to interpret what we find.

VERBAL GIVEAWAYS

In order to speak intelligently, we all have to collect our thoughts from time to time. When we're very familiar with the subject matter, very confident of ourselves, or especially at ease with the people we are conversing with, our words come easily. When a person is about to be deceptive, however, he needs a moment to think before speaking. Some distinct indicators of deception can result:

- hesitation before answering/speaking
- throat clearing
- stammering
- stuttering

One of the best opportunities we have for judging the truthfulness of another person is when we ask a question. Questions are powerful. Whether during casual conversation or more formal settings, questions allow us to fish for a response or pin a person down to a particular account. Simply the way a person responds to a query can offer up a wealth of information. It's been my experience that when a person answers a direct question in any of the following ways, there's an extreme likelihood of deception:

- repeats the question
- asks that the question be repeated
- asks a question back, rather than answering
- says, "What?"
- says, "What do you mean?"
- says, "Who me?"

These responses buy time when the recipient of the question is unable to easily come up with an answer. If "Where did you go last night?" is answered with "Where did I go last night?" we should wonder, "Why the stall?" Unless two people are in a loud environment that keeps a question from being clearly heard, there's no reasonable explanation for such a response. A person with honest intentions would simply answer the question.

I once interrogated a theft suspect who left me with a perfect example of this phenomenon. We were 20 minutes into the interrogation. It was perfectly quiet. Only the two of us were present. In a clear voice I asked him, "Did you steal the stereo?" Sitting only three feet from me, as we looked eye to eye the young man answered, "Who me?" I thought I'd heard everything!

People under stress don't consider whether their responses sound ridiculous. They fear silence more than they fear saying something stupid! They will impulsively speak just to fill the dead air, and they'll fill it with something incredibly telling.

RED FLAGS

There are certain phrases that often earmark a deceptive statement. Sometimes they're used to qualify an assertion, to make a denial sound more credible, or to avoid repeating a previous lie:

- You may not believe this, but...
- I won't deny I've done some things in the past, but I didn't do this...
- To the best of my knowledge...
- ...that I know of.
- I swear...
- Frankly...
- Really...
- Honestly...
- To be honest...
- To tell you the truth...
- Why would I do that?

- Do you believe me?
- Do I look like I would do something like that?
- Do you think I would do something like that?
- Do I look like the kind of person who would do that?
- I wasn't raised that way...
- I have no reason to lie to you...

Because people have a natural aversion to speaking a lie, they prefer to simply point back to one rather than repeat it.   Lying is risky, requires some effort, and creates discord with our internal moral code. Too, there's the fear of misstating a lie while repeating it.   Remarks generated from imagination are forgotten more quickly than are remarks generated from experience.   Repeating a lie the same way twice can be difficult.   The deceptive person, to avoid that stress, will often use responses like these:

- "I've already told you..."
- "Like I told you before..."
- "We've already covered this..."
- "How many times do I have to say this..."
- "I'm not going to go through it again..."

I'D LIKE TO, BUT MY POLICY OF DECEPTION WON'T ALLOW ME...

Sometimes the deceptive person expresses his "desire" to help with the truth:

- "That's all I can tell you." (because I don't want to get to the truth)

- "All I can say is..." (because I can't come up with anything better)

- "I wish I could tell you more." (but the truth is all that's left to say)

- "I would say..." (this is what I'll *say*—but it's not necessarily the truth)

- "I'll tell you this..." (because this is what I hope you'll believe)

These remarks are often used to explain the speaker's lack of a valuable answer. From an unconscious level, he's actually pointing out that the information he's giving is suspiciously narrow in scope—so obviously narrow that he feels obligated to address its shortcomings.

DISCLAIMERS

Disclaimers are great indicators of deception because they're acknowledgments from the speaker himself that what he's saying doesn't sound reasonable. Lines like these nearly always indicate deception:

- "I know this sounds strange, but..."
- "You may not believe this, but..."
- "You're going to think I'm making this up, but..."
- "This is even hard for me to believe, but..."
- "This is going to sound like a lie, but..."

Openers like these separate the speaker from his own statement. He has such little confidence in how what he's about to say will sound that he really doesn't want to be associated with it. By prefacing it with one of these dandy disclaimers, he's actually preparing us for the absurdity of the lie we're about to be handed.

INVOCATIONS

It's common in police interrogations to hear a suspect invoke his upbringing, sense of decency, or dead relatives in an effort to gain credibility for his claims of innocence. Many a suspect has sworn his story was the truth, "On my kid's life!" Would a guilty man do that? Absolutely! He'll say anything, do anything, to save his hide. The possibility of prison doesn't keep people from breaking laws, but it pushes the instinct of self-preservation to new levels when they've been caught. Some examples of invocations I've heard:

- "I swear on my (father's, mother's, son's, daughter's) grave."
- "I come from a decent family."
- "My mother didn't raise a thief."
- "I've always tried to stay out of trouble."
- "I always try to do right."
- "You can ask anybody and they'll tell you I wouldn't do something like that."

Such statements are warning bells. If you say you're a rebel, then you're not one. People who feel they need these kinds of invocations to enhance their believability have something to hide.

...

It should be apparent by now that the words people use often tell us more than the person speaking them realizes. The words people use are always what they want us to *accept* as the truth; it's up to us to determine whether they actually *are* the truth. Often, the deceptive person delivers his remarks in a package that, while designed to make his words more believable, actually reveals their deceit.

Finding Their True
Mental State

"What goes up must come down," and we can proclaim with equal certainty that "what is concealed on the inside must come out." Holding back on the truth creates anxiety and stress. Stress, we know, usually finds a way to manifest itself.

However it may have been learned, everyone knows that there is both an expectation of and an obligation to the truth. When a person becomes deceptive, his behavior violates that societal expectation. It's not through a sense of guilt, but rather a sense of incongruity that he feels anxious over his deception.

There are still others, who measure smaller in number, who

are drawn to truthfulness not so much by some moral or societal obligation, as by the fact that they fear the consequences of not telling the truth. People with this make-up find it easier to be deceptive because for them honesty is situational. If telling the truth seems more dangerous, they lie. If lying seems more dangerous, they tell the truth. Because avoiding consequences is their foremost concern, they go the direction that poses the least immediate threat. If Richard is questioned about the $500.00 he stole from his boss's cash register, he will likely regard telling the truth as posing the greatest threat to his self-interest. He'll choose to be deceptive, rather than follow some moral obligation to honesty.

As will be the case with the deceptive person who feels stress because his behavior is at odds with societal expectations, Richard's fear, too, will become the fear of being caught. That fear generates symptoms of deception.

Newton's Third Law of Motion states that "for every action there is an equal and opposite reaction." With regard to detecting deception, there happens to be an analogy for this: the more one goes in the direction of misrepresenting the truth, the more he will exhibit physical symptoms that indicate he's doing just that.

It's often the by-products of wrongdoing that get us caught, not the act itself. Few criminals are apprehended during the commission of a crime. It's fingerprints, DNA matches, phone records, murder weapons, bank records, and other peripheral evidences that lead crooks to their snaring. Similarly, it's the physical evidence of deception that leads us to recognize the person who is untruthful.

A friend of mine once shared with me that he had discovered a technique for determining if he were being watched. "I figured it out when I was in the library one day," he told me. "I had this funny feeling that this girl a few tables over was watching me, but I wasn't sure—every time I glanced up to catch her, she was looking another direction. Then I got an idea. I went back to reading my book, just minding my own business, and in a few minutes I pretended to yawn. I gave it about five seconds and looked at her again. She was yawning!"

My friend was no student of body language, but he had inadvertently stumbled onto something that most people never do. He discovered that people's intentional physical actions don't always match their true mental state, while their *unintended* physical actions always give it away.

Disingenuousness

Being a police detective in a 60-man department allowed me a great deal of latitude. With just five investigators, we lacked the luxury of specializing in particular crimes, rather, we each got a little of everything. From the standpoint of experience, that turned out to be a tremendous benefit for me; a forged check today, a double murder tomorrow. Each detective had his own preferences, but certainly none of us looked forward to the cases that involved children.

When I think of the characteristics that earmark the disingenuous person, I think of a man I dealt with on such a case in 1992. The mother of two elementary-age sisters had come forward to allege that this man had molested her daughters. As is common, he was a trusted family friend. He dropped by to check on them after school each afternoon. Sometimes he took them to get milk shakes, to the park, and other places before Mom came home at 5:30 each evening. She was aware of his looking after the girls, but was seemingly shocked when she learned there was more to the story than good-uncle favors.

I determined this man's work schedule and one evening parked down the block from his mother's house, where he lived also. I saw him arrive right on time and moments later I was knocking on his door. When he opened it, I introduced myself and asked if he would mind taking a ride with me to the police station. He extended his hand and I shook it. "There's something I'd like to get your side of," I told him. "Sure," he said with a broad smile. "Let me grab my keys."

If a police detective knocked on your door today and asked you to join him for a ride downtown, what would you say? What if he topped the invitation off with, "There's something I'd like to get your side of?" What would you do first: get your keys, or ask, "What's this about?" An innocent person (and granted, even some guilty ones) would immediately ask questions. The fact that this guy didn't need to question my purpose said everything. He knew what he had done, so my presence seemed reasonable to him.

The next red flag was his unbridled exuberance. I had to wonder if he'd just won the lottery! When he should have been relaxing with *Wheel of Fortune* and a TV dinner, he was instead being driven to the police department, apparently for questioning, and he seemed delighted to be doing it. Even as I steered the car onto the lot of the station, he still hadn't bothered to ask why I wanted to speak with him. But he talked about everything else. He had questions about the car. He asked about my job, how I liked it, how long I'd been at it. He told me about his job. He was polite, smiling the whole time. By the time I turned the car off, he ranked as the friendliest guy I'd dealt with all day.

He was, at heart, a manipulator. He was trying to use the same approach on me that he used on the two girls. He realized that being nice gets you further than just about anything, that seduction is at the same time stronger and quieter than brute force.

During my interrogation of this man, though, his mood changed. Early on, he smiled pleasantly as he denied abusing the girls. But as we continued, he smiled less. The charismatic sheen was wearing off. Depression was surfacing. At one point he told me, "Sometimes that .44 magnum just starts looking like a big sleeping pill."

This man's behavior typified disingenuousness. He tried to portray himself as something he wasn't in hopes of endearing himself to me and extinguishing my suspicions of him. He tried to act friendly, untroubled, and cordial, just as he probably did with his co-workers, family, and neighbors. Actually, these attributes were not his at all. As the subject of the girls loomed heavier around him, his thoughts easily went to suicide, something he told me he had long contemplated—but was this merely an effort to gain sympathy from me, yet another act of manipulation?

There are those who will cloak their real feelings and motives in niceties. Asking ourselves these two questions will help sort the fraudulent people from the genuine ones:

1) Is their behavior consistent with the circumstances?
2) What underlying goals might they be hoping to advance?

In addition to patronization, poor eye contact can be a sign of disingenuousness. People who are forthright, honest, and confident of what they have to say will have no problem looking you in the eye when they speak. When someone continually fails to make eye contact in a conversation, you can conclude that at best they are intimidated or unsure of themselves, and at worst, disingenuous or deceptive.

The Eyes Strike Again

If you look at your face normally in the mirror, you will see white on either side of the colored portion of each eye. When a person is tentative about what they are saying, often we'll see the white appear also under the colored portion of each eye, as well as on the sides. The head tilts down slightly, the eyes rotate up in their sockets, and we have "the three whites of the eyes."

Though I've seen this described as strictly a sign of deception, it's been my experience that it has broader meaning. It indicates that the person, as a result of what he is saying, is under stress. He may not be totally confident of what he is saying. He may have doubts that the listener is going to find his words believable. It also may be that he is deceptive.

An ability to accurately assess the eye whites takes some time to develop. Fortunately, it can be seen quite often, both in people we deal with personally and in those on television. Most episodes of *60 Minutes,* for instance, contain at least one confrontational interview. The person being interviewed is typically in the awkward position of defending something or someone. Though many of these people appear confident, well-versed, and believable, almost invariably we can see white displayed under the center of each eye. When we see this, we can conclude at a minimum that: 1) the person does not have full confidence in what he is saying, or 2) the person is not sure his words will be accepted as truthful. Both can be by-products of deception.

The three whites of the eyes is an alert sign. It's valuable because it is so noticeable. You may spot it when other, more subtle symptoms of deception have escaped your attention. When you see it displayed, evaluate the topic of conversation, what is being said, and other indicators of deception to determine its cause.

Disinterest

Effective conversation depends upon our message getting through to another person. When a person displays one or more of these symptoms, it's time to consider that we are losing, or have lost, their interest:

- offers minimal eye contact
- leans away from you

- offers no questions on the subject you're speaking on
- has no comments of his own on the subject you're speaking on
- changes the subject to something unrelated

The appearance of disinterest serves as an alert. Recognized early, it becomes a tool for measuring how well we're connecting with the other person and allows time for correction when we're not doing so well at it.

The Nose Knows

When it comes to interpreting symptoms of a person's true mental state, this one is my favorite. It's entertaining to watch and it's one of the most reliable indicators of a person's feelings toward a statement or situation. Fortunately, the touching or rubbing of the nose is also the most common physical gesture people display.

So what does it mean when someone rubs their nose? "It itches," you might say. Of course, there are times when it means nothing more than that. Where words and gestures are concerned, we can never say that something has one meaning for all situations. The very fact that words and gestures have multiple meanings happens to be our whole point of study. The nose is of interest because it's the most stress sensitive point on the human body. Stress always finds it way to the surface, and the nose is one of the first places it manifests itself.

I had some unexpected fun with my knowledge of nose gestures while in the Missouri State Highway Patrol Academy. Though a lot of our daily activities during the six-month training involved physical activity, a large amount of our time was spent in the classroom, where long days often proved as tiring as the running. Virtually every subject imaginable relating to law enforcement was at least touched upon, and as an internationally accredited agency, the

Patrol is required to teach specific topics. Each instructor had his or her own favorite subjects and areas of expertise. Other subjects were generic enough that no instructor specialized in them.

As we sat through a presentation one afternoon, something caught my eye. The instructor rubbed his nose. A few minutes later he did it again. I continued to see the nose rubs, which always came immediately after he received a question from the gallery.

This instructor was lecturing from text that day, reciting some prescribed, generic course material. Judging by his strict adherence to the printed material, it seemed that the subject was one of which he had little background—a notion that was confirmed by his continual nose gestures.

During a break I alerted a few fellow recruits to watch for the nose rubs and told them what they were, signs of discomfort. The information really didn't impress them too much until the lecture resumed, and they put it to use.

It was like a ritual: a question is received, then silence fills the room. The instructor's head goes down, there's a long pause, and then suddenly he looks up. Then, just as he is about to speak...he rubs his nose!

Was this instructor uncomfortable? Yes. He was feeling the anxiety of trying to answer questions on unfamiliar material. Was he lying? No. Was he being deceptive? Only in the sense that he was trying to appear knowledgeable on a subject he was not.

Not surprisingly, there were other days that this instructor seldom, if ever, touched his nose. When speaking on topics in which he had more personal experience, he performed quite differently. He often moved away from the lectern, was open and lighthearted, spoke without notes, and fielded questions without long pauses, looking away, or...committing a nose gesture.

Some have described the nose gesture as a straightforward sign of lying or deception. But study and observation have convinced me that's not always the case. Rubbing the nose is simply evidence of stress.

People commonly rub their noses while laughing at a joke (because it may not have been too funny, but we feel obligated to laugh anyway), upon entering a crowded room (because we feel as if we're on-stage), or upon being introduced to someone new. The discomfort and stress of even the simplest of situations can be enough to make the nerves inside one's nose tingle, a calling to which we can't help but respond.

It's wonderful to have such a visible and reliable meter of someone's true mental state, but the greatest value of a nose rub is realized when we can determine its cause. Is it the ex-spouse entering the room? Did the last question catch the person off-guard? Maybe the answer is in the words just spoken by the nose-rubber himself. Context always holds the answer. Suppose you ask your neighbor his opinion of the color of your new car, and he says, "It's great" and rubs his nose. You should consider that he isn't wild about it. If he later says, "I've seen a lot of those in blue," that might indicate he prefers blue over the color you selected.

It should be remembered that nose gestures always begin with momentary stress, a standard independent of deception. The situations in which people will be uncomfortable, unsure, embarrassed, or unaccepting will surely outnumber those where they'll be deceptive.

Rejection

It's been said that fear of failure keeps more people from succeeding than anything else. Our fear of failure is eclipsed only by our fear of rejection. It can be said that fear of failure is to professional endeavors, as fear of rejection is to personal ones.

But there's another kind of rejection, one that we fear less, yet experience more than personal rejection. It is the rejection of what we say. Whether it's the general subject we're speaking on or our specific take on an issue, it's critical to be able to recognize when another person is rejecting our statements:

- avoids eye contact
- turns body at an angle away from you
- faces you when speaking, but turns away when you speak
- creates a physical barrier between the two of you
- creates physical distance between the two of you
- crosses arms tightly
- diverts to a project, such as grinding out a cigarette or fiddling with something insignificant
- commits a nose gesture

Words have little effect when their target is in a state of rejection. When we sense rejection, its degree should dictate our course. Some mild signs of rejection sometimes appear when the parties aren't familiar or when an uncomfortable or a serious topic is mentioned. Backing away from the subject a bit, softening the approach, changing the subject temporarily, or revisiting previous topics that were successful are all remedies.

It's always valuable to identify the source of rejection. What was the remark, proposal, or action that immediately preceded the display of rejection? The source is usually obvious—it's always worth remembering for the moment, and sometimes for the future as well.

12

The Truth

My education on dealing with people has been both informal and formal. As a young police officer I was surrounded on a daily basis by a continual parade of miscreants, outlaws, and good hardworking citizens, a disproportionate mix of every element. The streets and alleys of my hometown were my laboratory, and those people were my unintended guinea pigs. I learned volumes from them, even if it might have taken me years to discern just what that knowledge is. Every cop has the same pool of resources I had, if he or she will make use of them. In fact, anyone who will bother to pay close attention to the people around them and how they behave has resources of a similar kind.

What I learned in classrooms, lectures, and seminars, I put to work on the streets and in the interrogation room. I found things that worked miraculously and things that worked only theoretically. I learned what I know not from seeing new things and drawing instant conclusions, but from seeing the same things over and over and drawing thoughtful conclusions. I'll freely admit that there have been plenty of times I was slow to learn. It was through repetition that I came to understand the significance of things that I—and everyone else—considered insignificant, or worse yet, hadn't considered at all. Learning didn't always mean finding something new, it meant finding the meaning of what I already knew.

Discovery is seeing what everybody else has seen, and thinking what nobody else has thought.

—Albert Szent-Gyorgi

Bandit's Quicksand

One spring afternoon in 1992, I was sitting in my office thinking about the business of crime and its antidotes. I had just wrapped up another burglary case. Two suspects, two confessions, the ideal way to clear a case from the books. As I considered how many cases we resolved just through the words of people, one of those thoughtful conclusions landed on me. I realized that there are essentially three ways a criminal can evolve into a suspect:

1) he can be caught in the act
2) he can implicate himself
3) another person can implicate him

The more I considered this the more obvious it seemed.

Every suspect I'd dealt with had taken his fall because at least one of these three conditions had come about.

While it may be his biggest fear, especially in the midst of pulling his caper, being caught in the act isn't the crook's biggest threat. The fact that very few people are caught for their first crime (in the act or at any time) proves the odds are in favor of most anyone getting away with a single crime. Success for even the most undisciplined criminal usually comes with his first try at crime. It's interesting to contrast this with the plight of the American entrepreneur, who, unlike the criminal, often fails at his first endeavor. But as the entrepreneur increases his odds of success through persistence and repetition, the criminal is imperiled by these things. Jesse James. Clyde Barrow. Ted Bundy. These names are well known because they belonged to people who found success at crime, and continued until they met failure. Such is the case with virtually every criminal, well known or unknown to the public.

If he gets away from the scene of the crime unscathed—and that includes leaving no fingerprints or other evidence that will haunt him later—the criminal can still land himself in jail with his own words. The prisons are full of people who are there only because they made an admission or gave a confession. Many were only a suspect among several until they sat down with a cop that was good at interviewing. No evidence or witness can compare to the impact of a suspect's own acknowledgment of guilt, and there are a surprising number of people who will give the police their confession. I've found most will even autograph it when asked nicely.

The third category probably accounts for more arrests of criminals than any other. If a bandit is fortunate enough to not be captured as he commits a crime and is smart enough not to confess to the police, then he's likely done something else just as hazardous to his freedom: allowed another person to have knowledge of his guilt.

This information of guilt can come about through any of several avenues. For instance, many crimes inherently require the involvement of more than one person. Drug trafficking is an example, a criminal enterprise that demands its participants know each other's identities and stand face to face as they conduct business. This leaves a lot of witnesses in the wake. I've known a few people in the drug trade who were exceedingly shrewd in the way they conducted their affairs. They treated it like a business and they made profits. They were successful for a while. By their own actions they would have never been caught. But the nature of their chosen business demanded that they deal with people less prudent. People who forego strategy and forethought meet failure more frequently than those who don't. In the drug trade this means that when the sloppy ones get caught, the dominoes start toppling. Informants are born. Plea bargains are struck. Eventually everyone is taken out, including those who did their level best to operate wisely. The truth, it seems, always finds its way to the surface—even if it takes a while.

Opinion, Fact, And Truth

There are few things that can never be taken from you, and opinions are one of them. Like ideas, thoughts, and beliefs, opinions also vary from one person to the next. Opinions are personal, and they are subjective. Each of us can have our own opinions, reasonable or otherwise. And though they can surely be influenced, they are ultimately ours to do with as we choose.

Fact, on the other hand, is owned by no one. It is fact that oxygen is in the air we breathe. It is fact that rain is water. Unlike opinion, fact is objective. It is constant from one person to the next.

Truth is merely an accurate and honest translation of fact conveyed to others. Thinking back to our discussion of recollection and construction, you'll remember that when a person's eyes go in the direction of recollection, they are retrieving factual information. I noted that because it is factual, it is also truthful. Truth is an *extension* of fact, a mere recitation of it.

Theories and definitions are great, but we know that not everyone is guided by them. If everyone made it habit to relate only fact when they presented "the truth," you would have never picked up this book. Sometimes what is presented as truth is not a recitation of fact, but the speaker's translation of fact. Certain points have been omitted, shined up, or adjusted to better suit the speaker's interests.

Rather than giving fabricated-from-scratch lies, most people who are deceptive will give an edited version of the truth. The teller wants to stay as close to truth as is allowable, while still satisfying the objectives that led him to be deceptive. People want to use the least degree of deception possible.

Why is it they don't want to leave the truth behind entirely? One reason is that running parallel to the truth allows them to grab hold of it again if the need arises. Frequently, we find that in order to stay close to the truth, yet still misrepresent fact, people mingle opinion and truth. If caught, they have some fact to cite in their defense. Another reason for staying close to the truth is that deception, lying especially, is hard work. People don't look for reasons to be deceptive, and they'd rather not. Situations always arise, though, where it becomes "necessary."

In Chapter 10, I noted that "I think" and "I believe" are phrases that, while intended to reinforce a statement, often actually undermine it. Only "I know," which is usually implied, not spoken, demonstrates relation of truth:

"I think"   reflects OPINION
"I believe"   reflects OPINION
"I know"   reflects TRUTH

It's worth noting that "I think" and "I believe" have different implications depending on whether the speaker is discussing opinion or fact. When a person speaks about his ideas, philosophies, beliefs, or similar subjects, he is not referencing fact, he's referencing his opinion. The terms "I think" and "I believe" are appropriate to use when a person is stating his own viewpoints and shouldn't be construed to indicate deception.

It's when these two phrases are used to comment upon fact that they can tell us something more. They usually indicate one of two things when a person uses them in discussing fact: 1) they innocently question their own recollection of fact, or 2) they are intentionally misrepresenting fact.

It's true that occasionally people have a hard time remembering. It's happened to all of us. Despite our best efforts at recollection, sometimes what we recollect is hazy or piecemeal. We aren't trying to be deceptive, we just can't completely remember. Using "I think" or "I believe" while discussing an issue of fact may be the person's honest way of telling us they are recalling as best they can but are unsure of their accuracy.

On the other hand, a person who is intentionally misrepresenting fact may also use either of the two phrases. We saw an example of this when we examined Mr. Hoover's statement, "We have the right people, I think."

Since both honest and deceptive people use these phrases, we obviously need some way of sorting the bad from the good. Is the person signaling his innocent doubt about his own recollection? Is he tempering his assertion of fact, which would indicate deception? Probably the best way to judge which is the case is to notice where the terms are placed in a sentence. Used at the beginning of a sentence, these words indicate sincere doubt about the speaker's own recollection.

- "I believe it was on a Tuesday."

Used at the end, they temper his assertion of fact:

- "It was on a Tuesday, I believe."

Notice how frequently politicians say "I think" when they speak. Because what someone "thinks" has no objective provability, the term gives them shelter. To the sharp listener, however, their overuse of this phrase illustrates their lack of commitment to, or lack of confidence in what they are saying.

The strongest statements regarding fact contain neither "I think," nor "I believe." Unless the person is citing poor memory, which is not commonly the case, "I think" has no place in a statement of fact. If a person came indoors from a rainstorm he wouldn't likely say, "I think it's raining," or even, "I believe it's raining." He would say, "It's raining." Truth needs no support, no qualification.

Removing "I think" and "I believe" from our own speech will demonstrate we have confidence in what we say. Saying, "This will be the best plan" is more powerful than, "This will be the best plan, I think." Declaratory statements that include "I think" or "I believe" not only point out the subjectivity of the statement, but the "I" introduces the person into the discussion. Our statements have greater likelihood of being accepted when we portray them as objective fact rather than subjective opinion, and keep ourselves separate from the issue.

Where Influence, Opinion, And Truth Meet

Unlike opinion, truth is universal among people, constant from one person to the next. When it comes to influencing others, though, there's a stark difference between influencing a person's statement of opinion and influencing their statement of fact. On which of these two positions do you think a person would more easily reverse himself:

- "Hunter would be a strong governor."
- "I went to Ted's house last night."

The first statement concerns opinion, the second one fact. Because opinion is theoretically neither right nor wrong, it can be changed (albeit most people are stubborn in doing it), with no reflection on the honesty of the person who holds the opinion.

Changing one's position on fact, though, is a different matter. This is so because fact is not changeable. If a person changed "I didn't go to Ted's house last night," to "I went to Ted's house last night," we would have to conclude that one of the statements had been deceptive. Because it will be a reflection on one's honesty, it's much tougher to get a person to change his position on fact than opinion.

People do sometimes change their position on fact (which means they have been deceptive). This typically occurs when they have been pressed into a corner and have no remaining alternatives. They may sense they aren't believed. The questions may be getting tougher to field. Perhaps they are confronted head-on with undeniable truth. When a deceptive person who finds himself in such circumstances wants to do an about-face with his position on fact, how will he do it so as to preserve his appearance of honesty? He'll cite his faulty recollection, of course. Lines such as "I forgot," or "I was thinking of a different time," are likely to be brandished on occasions like these.

This is why lines like "I don't remember," or "not that I can think of," are worth noting. People use phrases like these to "hedge a lie." If they're cornered into changing their position on a fact later, lines like these allow them to call their previous statements mistakes and themselves victims of faulty recollections.

Understanding The Goals Of Deception

To know truth, we must know deception. To that end, virtually all study on the subject of deception—including this book— focuses on *how* it is carried out. What does it look like? What does it sound like? What are the characteristics and subtleties that will expose it?

If we work hard enough at learning to recognize deception, sooner or later we will. At the point we decide another person is deceptive, our attention will suddenly shift away from *how* the deception was carried out. The work will be done. The evidence that led us to the decision will take a back seat to the realization that the person with whom we're conversing chose not to be truthful with us. No one wants to be duped. Regardless of the circumstances, our first reaction will be offense.

If we're going to put great effort into recognizing deception, it's certainly worthwhile to step back and take a look at the reasons *why* deception is carried out. Perhaps with a little understanding of what motivates people to be deceptive, we can avoid falling prey to the emotional reaction that so often follows finding it. It has been my experience that there are three reasons for deception: self-preservation, fraud, and pathology.

SELF-PRESERVATION

The overwhelming majority of people who choose to be deceptive do so out of necessity. This isn't to say that they are justified in committing their deception, only that circumstances, typically of their own creation, have placed them in the position of needing to use deception to avoid a perceived greater negative.

The average person doesn't enjoy being deceptive. He doesn't look for reasons to be deceptive. To the contrary, he looks for alternatives to deception. This is evidenced by the fact that people who do resort to deception almost invariably start with the least amount that will suffice, then progress if needed:

1) avoidance
2) omission
3) lying

These fall under the broad umbrella of deception, and they increase in terms of risk and commitment from #1 to #3. If at all possible, a person who is in the position of being deceptive would rather avoid giving an answer than generate a lie, and he would rather omit a damaging detail than lie.

Though people have a natural aversion to lying, most will do it if the truth poses enough jeopardy to their well-being. Self-preservation is one of our most fundamental instincts, and it will lead otherwise honorable and well-meaning people to employ deception.

FRAUD

Though it may not be prevalent, fraud as a motivation for deception is worth noting because it presents a much greater danger than does either self-preservation or pathology. This is true because a person who is motivated by fraud is typically trying to perpetrate a scheme upon the listener. It may be something as relatively innocuous as a person saying the odometer on the car he's trying to sell represents the vehicle's actual mileage when the true mileage is much more. It may be a politician misrepresenting his opponent's position on an issue. It may be a Gypsy in a parking lot telling an elderly person he'll split "found" money with him, so long as the old man puts up a good faith deposit.

Whatever the purpose, a person motivated by fraud is typically trying to put something over on the listener. Unlike self-preservation, which is a defensive maneuver, fraud has a forward objective. While deception for the sake of self-preservation usually concerns past events, deception for fraud centers on future objectives that benefit the deceptive person.

When someone tries to deceive us for the purpose of fraud, we're justified in feeling anger; their objective is to mislead us in hopes of fulfilling their self-serving causes.

PATHOLOGY

There are those who gravitate without cause to lying. Because they lack that natural aversion to deception that most people possess, they don't bother with avoidance or omission. They begin with lying.

If you've ever dealt with a pathological liar you know how astonishing it can be to realize that another person is lying to you with no purpose. And motivation is precisely what sets the pathological liar apart from the other two categories. People propelled by pathology have no apparent objectives—precisely the reason the pathological liar is so maddening to deal with.

...

None of us like the feeling we get when a person denies us the truth. I remember being in interrogations where I knew that the person was lying to me. I must admit that it angered me, even if I didn't let it show.

Were these people acting out of self-preservation, fraud, or pathology? When I stopped to consider it, I realized that the people who were deceptive with me in interrogations were motivated by self-preservation. They weren't trying to damage me by perpetrating an overt scheme—they were trying to defend themselves by evading the consequences of their actions. But when they lied to me, it felt personal. This illustrates just how powerful emotions are in conversation. Regardless of what inspires a person's deception, on the receiving end it always feels like fraud.

Reliables And Remedies

Because no two conversations are exactly alike, there is no universal formula for success that will provide for all occasions. Getting positive results from conversation is more complicated than that, of course. Part of the challenge, part of the fun of this sport, though, lies in that intrinsic unpredictability.

Most of us find out sooner or later that learning how to do something is far different from actually doing it. Absorbing information may be tedious or time consuming, but over the course of trying to implement it, we usually come to reflect on the study as having been the easy part.

The Five Reliables

Situations will vary, but there are several dynamics we can rely upon that will help us understand what moves people to say what they do in conversation. All will work to the advantage of anyone who will recognize them.

PEOPLE TALK TOO MUCH

There are two sides to every story and two sides to every conversation. When a person speaks, he's giving up information. When he listens, he's taking it in. Which will be more advantageous? On which side of conversation do you want to spend the most time?

Even as we ask a question, we're revealing information. A question reveals what we already know, exposes just what we don't know, and gives the listener a clear view of where our interests lie. Ideally, whatever information we give up as we ask a question is more than compensated by the information it elicits.

But it's talking, not questions, that is normally the problem. Our words—even when we're not asking a question—should be designed to get the other person to give away more information than we do. Usually we don't need to ask questions to achieve this. People will generally tell us what they know if we'll simply get out of the way and let them do it.

PEOPLE WANT TO TELL WHAT THEY KNOW

Hells Angels have a saying: "Three can keep a secret if two are dead." The human inclination to tell what we know is overwhelming. How many times has a person said to you, "Now don't repeat this, but...." They themselves were undoubtedly told not to repeat the information, but the admonishment didn't hold, did it? Why? Because people want to tell what they know. The more tawdry and scandalous the tidbit, the faster it moves through the circuit of secrecy. Soon the information is secret in name only.

We shouldn't be flattered to be the one who is entrusted with such secrets. When we are tempted to confide in the teller, we should realize it cuts both ways; we should expect him to divulge our confidences just as easily.

PEOPLE TELL THE TRUTH

People want to be truthful, and they almost always are. The human inclination toward truthfulness is so strong that even as a person is being deceptive, he will still do his best to stay truthful. Can a person be truthful and deceptive at the same time? Absolutely. This can be best illustrated through a statement made by a suspect in an internal theft case: "I inventoried the diamonds, put the case in the safe, and left." That sounds like a straightforward statement, doesn't it? The inference is that this person put the diamonds in the case—but notice he didn't say that.

Nothing in the statement is a lie. He inventoried the diamonds. He put the case in the safe. He left. Everything in the statement actually happened, it's just that he left out another thing that happened, his removal of the diamonds from the case. Though deceptive by design, this statement is technically truthful.

The thief in this case did what many people do. By simply omitting a harmful truth, a person can deceive his listener and at the same time avoid the discomfort that comes with creating a lie.

It is always good policy to tell the truth—unless, of course, you are an exceptionally good liar.

—Jerome K. Jerome

Avoidance is the pre-eminent manifestation of the human tendency toward truth, and is most often used in response to a direct question. Answers such as "Why do you ask," "Who me?"

and "Why would I do that?" not only buy time for thought, but they allow the answerer to reply without lying. Of course, a person's lack of an answer speaks for itself.

Lying is hard to bring oneself to do, and it's hard to bring off. People use it only as a last resort.

EVERYTHING PEOPLE SAY HAS MEANING

Everything that comes out of a person's mouth is produced through either: 1) choice, or 2) accident. In either case, the words will have meaning. Statements produced through choice contain the information that a person consciously chooses and wants us to accept. But the majority of information transmitted by people falls into the category of "accidental" information (though most listeners fail to recognize it). A person's use of phrases such as "To tell you the truth," and "I think" are not intended to convey information to the listener, but of course, we know they do. Because they deliver information that the speaker didn't intend, these kinds of phrases are accidental.

Similarly, people often include words or subjects in conversation that appear insignificant or irrelevant. Anytime we hear a person speak words that seem insignificant or irrelevant, we must immediately consider them to be significant and relevant. Because words have meaning—regardless of whether the speaker realizes he is revealing the information—words or subjects that seem out of place must be carefully considered.

To their own detriment, people typically focus on the obvious information they are given in conversation. The shortcoming of that information is that the speaker was quite cognizant of its content and likely filtered or adjusted it accordingly. To the contrary, the words and phrases that people least consider are the ones which are most revealing.

PEOPLE WANT TO BE RIGHT

In Chapter 4 I noted that when our beliefs, statements, or proposals are under attack we usually end up on the defensive side of an argument. This happens because the ego doesn't like defeat, and failing to answer the disparagement of what we have said feels a lot like losing. The thought of not defending oneself in conversation seems more distasteful than the oncoming argument.

Even in a conversation where there is argument, there will be occasions when the other side makes a statement that agrees with our position, if only on a minor point. When this happens, we might instinctively announce, "That's what I've been saying!" Why? Because we want to be right.

But instead of proclaiming that *we* are right, when they make a statement that supports our case we should proclaim that the *other party* is right. Though it rarely is achieved, the distant goal of argument is to hear one's adversary say, "You're right." So when the other person agrees with any part of what you have said, stifle the ego and tell him, "You're right." Because people hear "You're right" so infrequently, a person who is granted this acknowledgment will be drawn closer to the point that elicited it and closer to your case.

The Five Simple Remedies

We can't prepare for future conversations specifically, but there are some habits we can develop which will equip us to navigate more effectively in conversations when they come, truthful or otherwise.

ASK QUESTIONS

Curiosity is in scarce supply these days—perhaps it always has been. Curiosity killed the cat, but it also invented the airplane, the light bulb, and the transistor radio.

A lack of curiosity may be another explanation why most

people talk predominately about their own thoughts and experiences. It's partly due to an egocentric approach to life, but it's due also to a lack of real curiosity. A person with a low level of curiosity won't ask many questions—the result will be many missed learning opportunities.

Curiosity is one of the most permanent and certain characteristics of a vigorous intellect.

—Samuel Johnson

Even when they are curious, some people are simply reluctant to ask questions. Perhaps they don't want to pry, don't want to offend, or are afraid of potential answers. Incredibly, it has been estimated that some 90% of salesmen never ask the prospect if he wants to buy! It would be staggering to know the number of sales that are missed every day simply because salesmen didn't ask this elementary and reasonable question.

Curiosity is vital, and questions harness it. Questions not only bring information back, but because the person asking questions is the one in control of a conversation, they allow one to subtly command the course of conversation.

STAY FLEXIBLE

People inherently want to find what works and then stick with it. Adaptation goes against our grain. Staying flexible is something that even veteran interrogators can find difficult. A friend of mine tells the story of a seasoned interrogator who had progressed to become an instructor in the art. To the police officers who attended his presentations, he recommended a singular approach: walk into the room with a large file, slam it down on the table, tell the suspect you know he's guilty and that he's going to prison for a long time. After the gravity of the situation has sunk in, he suggested that the pressure be turned down and a remedy for the dilemma be made available: do the right thing, own up, give a confession. While this approach might elicit a confession from some suspects, it isn't flexible enough to account for differing personalities and differing circumstances, two factors we must accommodate in any conversation.

Flexibility doesn't come naturally to us. Whatever the endeavor, we find a way that's comfortable and we cling to it, even though the approach may work only a percentage of the time. We focus on our occasional successes as confirmation that we have a winning plan, though behind us is a trail strewn with missed opportunities.

If it works we'll claim that we planned it all along.
—Billy Gibbons

We do ourselves a great service when we stay open to new ways and refuse to believe we've found the only way.

GIVE LOGIC MORE AUTHORITY THAN EMOTION

Where conversation is concerned, emotion leads to defeat. It makes us argumentative, stubborn, rude, and shortsighted. We trade the momentary satisfaction of a sharp comeback for the deeper, long term objectives that would benefit us most. Of everything covered, eliminating emotional reactions is the single most difficult thing described here, especially in personal conversations. It's also the most critical.

Nothing gives one person so much advantage over another as to remain always cool and unruffled under all circumstances.
—Thomas Jefferson

Emotion blurs judgment. It's the cause of marriages and the cause of divorces. It brings friends together and it sends them apart for life. The most insidious part of emotion is that it leads us to make momentary decisions that often have much farther reaching consequences than just the moment. Days, months, or years later, we may think differently about hasty decisions made under the influence of emotion.

Logic seldom lets us down the way emotion can. Words, decisions, and actions generated through cool deliberation typically hold up better over time.

In the first chapter I mixed strategy with conversation; strategy is an end product of logic and both are needed to produce predictable results in conversation.

LISTEN

Because people want to tell what they know, and because they are mostly truthful, we can glean volumes of information simply by listening. People fail to appreciate listening as a tool, behaving as if speaking were the only thing that could benefit them in dealing with others. While we consider what to say next, or while we say it, tremendous amounts of information escape us.

Information escapes us, and so does *absence* of information. Since avoidance is the pre-eminent form of deception, difficult questions frequently go "unanswered." Just as frequently, the person who asked the question is distracted by the "answer" and fails to recognize that the original question went unaddressed. Always keep mental track of the question you've asked as you listen to a person's response. Then ask yourself, "Did he answer it?" The lack of an answer should be interpreted as a symptom of deception. In social or personal settings, the question should be subtly revisited later. In formal question-and-answer settings, the question should be immediately repeated, disallowing the recipient the luxury of evasion.

EMPOWER YOURSELF THROUGH PATIENCE AND FORESIGHT

Some folks possess natural talent for conversation, and likewise at influencing the beliefs of others. Jim Jones, David Koresh, and Bill Clinton all were gifted with such talent. But regardless of talent level, we each improve at any endeavor with practice. Baseball great George Brett and record-breaking golfer Tiger Woods no doubt were gifted with natural abilities. To be at the top of their sports, though, they still found it necessary to develop their skills through relentless practice.

Rome wasn't built in a day—and neither was Syracuse.
—Shemp Howard

At the writing of this book, the United States economy is arguably as good as it has ever been. Inflation is non-existent, interest rates are near all time lows, and unemployment is a problem of the past. But consumer debt is overflowing. This is largely due to an incredible upsurge in credit card usage. The average household now bears an estimated $6,000.00 in credit card debt.

This can be explained in large part by a lack of patience and foresight on the part of many credit card users. First, they lack the patience to wait until they can afford to pay cash for a particular item and credit cards allow them to spend the money they've yet to make. Second, they lack the foresight to envision the consequences of racking up long-term debt.

Patience and foresight are two characteristics that lead to

solid decision making in any pursuit. In conversation they become especially powerful. Patience enables us to learn the intricacies of deceptive behavior. Foresight allows us to ignore the momentary temptations that stand to rob us of greater outcomes ahead.

Turn Right To Go Left

On my office wall I have a framed black and white photograph of a
street sign. I spotted it one day as I drove down an Omaha,
Nebraska boulevard riddled with orange cones and construction
barricades. It was a temporary sign that bore the words, "Turn
Right To Go Left." Instead of simply turning left across the path of
oncoming traffic, drivers wishing to go that direction had to first
turn right and go around a small concrete island, whereupon they
could cross the street when the light turned green. The sign looked
like a question mark without a period at the bottom and had an

arrow at the top that pointed left.

I stopped when I saw that sign and snapped a picture of it. It was a strange and unexpected symbol of everything I had come to learn about influence and deception. I've come to know that, ironically, getting the most out of people and their words usually means taking the less direct and less obvious routes.

Placement Equals Results

Self-defense experts will tell you that if you're going to have a gun for personal protection, the absolute minimum caliber to have is .380. Anything less, they say, can't be depended upon to do the job—and they're right. But in the summer of 1993, I worked a shooting in which a healthy, muscular, 200 pound man was dropped by a single shot from a .25 caliber handgun. Not only is the .25 a lesser gun than the .380, but it's also the least powerful weapon on the market.

That guy never got up again. The slowest moving, least respected bullet money could buy had slipped between two ribs on his left side, lumbered through one lung and the edge of his heart, and then lodged in his spine. Twelve hours later I was watching his autopsy. A piece of lead the size of a baby's big toe turned out to be equal to a full grown, tough-guy, crack dealer.

We can marvel, but we shouldn't be incredulous. A tiny bullet that hits the right spot will kill more reliably than will a shot to the foot from a deer rifle. Delivery is more powerful than substance. It's true with guns, it's true with words.

As I've pointed out in various ways, the *way* thoughts are said is always more powerful than *what* is said. The fact that delivery trumps everything else in conversation is what allows you to read the real meaning in what another person says, even when they'd rather have you believe something else. Likewise, packaging your thoughts the right way will cause others to have greater acceptance of your words.

Realizing there's more to conversation than most people appreciate is fifty percent of finding it. The second half—learning how to be proficient at influencing others and recognizing deception—is more time consuming (and more fun).

Yet, few bother to make it even half way. Appreciating the importance of how we present our thoughts, and how we interpret what others have presented to us, is something that most people never grasp in a lifetime. That's okay. Despite their loss, and on occasion even through their loss, fortunately, the rest of us will find continual opportunity.

Let us be thankful for the fools, but for them the rest of us could not succeed.

—Mark Twain

Index

WANT TO REACH THE AUTHOR?

cdauthor@hotmail.com